Mary Todd Lincoln

Mary Todd Lincoln

★★★★★★★★★★★★★★★★★★★★★★★

1818–1882

BY DAN SANTOW

CHILDREN'S PRESS®
A Division of Grolier Publishing
New York   London   Hong Kong   Sydney
Danbury, Connecticut

Consultant: LINDA CORNWELL
Learning Resource Consultant
Indiana Department of Education

Project Editor: DOWNING PUBLISHING SERVICES
Page Layout: CAROLE DESNOES
Photo Researcher: JAN IZZO

Visit Children's Press on the Internet at:
http://publishing.grolier.com

Library of Congress Cataloging-in-Publication Data
Santow, Dan.
    Mary Todd Lincoln, 1818–1882 / by Dan Santow
        p.   cm. — (Encyclopedia of first ladies)
    Includes bibliographical references and index.
    Summary: A biography of the wife of the sixteenth president of the United States,
discussing her upbringing, marriage, and the tragedies that marred her life.
    ISBN 0-516-20481-5
    1. Lincoln, Mary Todd, 1818–1882—Juvenile literature. 2. Presidents' spouses—United
States—Biography—Juvenile literature. [1. Lincoln, Mary Todd, 1818–1882 2. First ladies.
3. Women—Biography] I. Title II. Series.
E457.325.L55S25   1999
973.7'092—dc21   98–45254
[B]   CIP
                                                                   AC

Table of Contents

Mary Todd Lincoln

CHAPTER ONE

Mary Todd Lincoln's Worst Dream Comes True

✶ ✶ ✶ ✶ ✶ ✶ ✶ ✶ ✶ ✶ ✶ ✶ ✶ ✶ ✶

It was to have been the most lovely evening. So lovely, in fact, that Mary Todd Lincoln had begun to think of it as a second chance, a new beginning. The Civil War, which had raged and divided the country for more than four years, was finally over. The last battles had been fought—and won. The Union army was on its way home. So, Mary thought, was her husband, President Abraham Lincoln.

After all, she reasoned, the war had been grueling not only on the country, but on her family. But tonight, April 14, 1865, would be different. Tonight there would be a carriage ride through town, a light-

✶ ✶ ✶ ✶ ✶ ✶ ✶ ✶ ✶ ✶ ✶ ✶ ✶ ✶ ✶

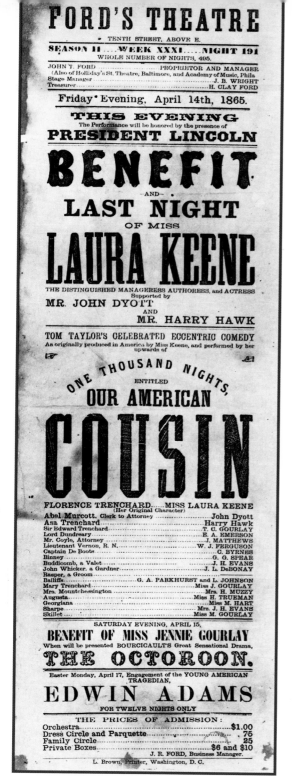

FORD'S THEATRE
• TENTH STREET, ABOVE E. •

SEASON II .... WEEK XXXI .... NIGHT 191
WHOLE NUMBER OF NIGHTS, 495.

JOHN T. FORD .... PROPRIETOR AND MANAGER
(Also of Holliday's St. Theatre, Baltimore, and Academy of Music, Phila
Stage Manager .... J. B. WRIGHT
Treasurer .... H. CLAY FORD

Friday • Evening, April 14th, 1865.

THIS EVENING
The Performance will be honored by the presence of
PRESIDENT LINCOLN

BENEFIT
—AND—
LAST NIGHT
OF MISS
LAURA KEENE

THE DISTINGUISHED MANAGERESS AUTHORESS, and ACTRESS
Supported by
MR. JOHN DYOTT
AND
MR. HARRY HAWK

TOM TAYLOR'S CELEBRATED ECCENTRIC COMEDY
As originally produced in America by Miss Keene, and performed by her
upwards of

ONE THOUSAND NIGHTS,
ENTITLED
OUR AMERICAN
COUSIN

FLORENCE TRENCHARD .... MISS LAURA KEENE
(Her Original Character)
Abel Murcott, Clerk to Attorney .... John Dyott
Asa Trenchard .... Harry Hawk
Sir Edward Trenchard .... T. C. GOURLAY
Lord Dundreary .... E. A. EMERSON
Mr. Coyle, Attorney .... J. MATTHEWS
Lieutenant Vernon, R. N. .... W. J. FERGUSON
Captain De Boots .... C. BYRNES
Binney .... G. G. SPEAR
Buddicomb, a Valet .... J. H. EVANS
John Whicker, a Gardner .... J. L. DeBONAY
Rasper, a Groom
Bailiff .... G. A. PARKHURST and L. JOHNSON
Mary Trenchard .... Miss J. GOURLAY
Mrs. Mountchessington .... Mrs. H. MUZZY
Augusta .... Miss H. TRUEMAN
Georgiana .... Miss M. HART
Sharpe .... Mrs. J. H. EVANS
Skillet .... Miss M. GOURLAY

SATURDAY EVENING, APRIL 15,
BENEFIT OF MISS JENNIE GOURLAY
When will be presented BOURCICAULT'S Great Sensational Drama,
THE OCTOROON.

Easter Monday, April 17, Engagement of the YOUNG AMERICAN
TRAGEDIAN,
EDWIN ADAMS
FOR TWELVE NIGHTS ONLY

THE PRICES OF ADMISSION :
Orchestra $1.00
Dress Circle and Parquette 75
Family Circle 25
Private Boxes .... $6 and $10
J. R. FORD, Business Manager.
L. Brown, Printer, Washington, D. C.

Clara Harris

*Left: A handbill advertising the play being
performed the evening President Lincoln was shot*

hearted play called *Our American
Cousin* at Ford's Theatre and much
carefree conversation. The only disap-
pointment, as far as Mary could tell,
was that General Ulysses Grant and
his wife, who were supposed to accompany them, had to cancel. Instead, the
Lincolns would share the presidential
box at the theater with Clara Harris,
the daughter of New York senator Ira
Harris, and her fiancé, Major Henry
Rathbone.

Ford's Theatre, scene of the assassination of President Abraham Lincoln, as it looks today

The stage of Ford's Theatre, with the presidential box on the right

Mary took great care in getting dressed that night, thoughtfully choosing a dramatic black-and-white-striped full-bodied dress. Lincoln, though, had been in long meetings all day. By the time he returned to the White House around seven in the evening, he was tired and suffering from a headache. But during dinner they decided to go to the theater, despite his discomfort. A comedy, a few hearty laughs, would be good for them both. And besides, their attendance had been advertised and the rest of the audience would be disappointed if they failed to show up.

So, around 8:15 that night, Lincoln, in a black overcoat and white gloves, and Mary in all her finery, got into their carriage for the short ride to the theater. It was foggy outside and cool, and the carriage moved slowly through the dark streets. Only the gaslights shimmered in the night.

They were late arriving at the theater and when they entered, the play was already in progress. Nevertheless, the orchestra started to play "Hail to the Chief."

As they made their way to their seats in the presidential box, the audience gave them a standing ovation. The box, which was festooned with two American flags flanking a portrait of George Washington, was

Popular actress Laura Keene starred in Our American Cousin

above and to the right of the stage. The star of the play, popular actress Laura Keene, looked up and curtsied to them. Lincoln sat in a comfortable rocking chair covered in red damask. Mary sat in a straight-backed chair at his side.

Mary rested her hand on Lincoln's knee. Later, he would take her hands in his and together they watched the play. "What will Miss Harris think of my hanging on to you so?" she whispered to Lincoln. "She won't think anything about it," he assured her. All in Mary's world seemed safe now, there in the cozy presidential box, holding hands with her husband. Their guard, John Parker, saw that the president and his wife and their guests were comfortable. He then left the box, closed the door without locking it, and disappeared.

Feeling safe—that's all Mary really craved. Safe from the troubles of the war. Safe from the death of any more of her children. Safe from money worries. Safe from the press, who had spent four years viciously attacking her for everything she did, no matter, it seemed, how minor.

During the third act of the play, as Lincoln and his wife continued to hold hands, a well-known actor named John Wilkes Booth quietly entered the presidential box. He was wearing a black felt hat and high boots with spurs. With the guard away, there was no one to stop him, no security for the president and his wife.

Within seconds, Booth pointed a gun directly at the president's head. And then he pulled the trigger. A shot rang out, echoing throughout the

Assassin John Wilkes Booth, wearing a black felt hat and high boots with spurs, entering the presidential box

John Wilkes Booth (1838–1865)

✦ ✦

The ninth-born of ten children in a family of famous actors in Maryland, young John Wilkes Booth spent little time in school. Though emotionally unstable, he eventually became a Shakespearean actor and made his debut in Baltimore at the age of seventeen. As the Civil War loomed, he strongly supported the Confederate cause. Just before war's end, he cooked up a far-fetched plan to kidnap President Lincoln and bargain his return for Northern surrender. The war ended before he could act, so he settled on assassination instead. After accomplishing the deed that fateful April night, he fled into the darkness. The War Department offered a $50,000 reward for his capture. Twelve days later, Union cavalry troops found him hiding in a barn in the Virginia countryside. Most accounts agree that he was killed by his captors. Some believe he committed suicide to avoid surrender. Although Booth's body was returned to Washington for autopsy and secret burial, for years the rumor persisted that he lived to wander through the Southwest as one John St. Helene. When St. Helene took his own life in 1903, people who believed him to be the assassin of President Lincoln preserved and exhibited his body to make a tidy profit.

Booth in the barn being captured

Booth jumped down from the president's box and fled across the stage after the shooting.

theater. A small cloud of misty smoke from the gunpowder quickly formed and then just as quickly drifted away. The bullet hit Lincoln behind his left ear, sped through his brain, and lodged behind his right eye.

Booth, who had supported the losing side in the war, leaped from the box where Mary and Lincoln were sitting to the stage below. But it wasn't a clean jump—one of his spurs got

The Plot Thickens

★ ★ ★ ★ ★ ★ ★ ★ ★ ★ ★ ★ ★ ★ ★ ★ ★ ★ ★ ★

The assassination of Lincoln was only part of the plot hatched by John Wilkes Booth for April 14. In the months before, Booth rounded up a ragtag band of rogues and ruffians who sided with the Confederacy. Together, they plotted to kill the president, Vice President Andrew Johnson, and Secretary of State William Seward at the same time. Booth, as we know, carried through his assignment successfully, but George Atzerodt lost his nerve and did not attack Johnson. Lewis Payne succeeded in knifing, though not killing, Seward, who lay in bed recovering from a carriage accident. Before April's end, seven of the known conspirators, including boardinghouse owner Mrs. Mary E. Surratt who "kept the nest where the egg was hatched," had been imprisoned. With swift justice, they were tried and convicted. Payne, Atzerodt, Surratt, and David Herold (who helped Booth escape after the shooting) were hanged on a blistering hot July 7, 1865, in the courtyard of Washington's Arsenal Penitentiary. Three others, along with Dr. Samuel Mudd, who had set Booth's broken leg, were condemned to hard labor at Fort Jefferson on the remote Dry Tortugas, a group of islands off Florida.

caught on the American flag hanging below the box. He hit the floor hard, breaking his left shinbone.

Many in the audience, utterly stunned and confused about what was happening, thought he was a part of the play. As he tumbled to the floor, some in the audience thought they heard him shout, "The South shall be free!" He ran, limping, from the stage.

"Stop that man!" someone shouted. "Stop that man! Won't somebody stop that man? The president is shot!"

Upon hearing this, people in the audience began to scream and move frantically about, trying to escape the theater and the horror that had just occurred. Some, including the actress on the stage, began to call for order. "For God's sake, have the presence of mind to keep your places," she shouted, "and all will be well!"

It had happened so fast and so unexpectedly that at first Mary didn't realize what had happened. Lincoln jerked forward and slumped. Screaming, Mary reached out instinctively to stop him from falling. But there was nothing she could do to save him.

Within moments, twenty-three-

Dr. Charles Leale, who had been in the audience, tried in vain to save the president.

year-old Charles Leale, a doctor who had been in the audience, rushed to the box and tried giving Lincoln mouth-to-mouth resuscitation. For a second it began to work. Though unconscious, Lincoln started to breathe on his own. "Oh, doctor! Is he dead?" Mary asked through her tears, "Can he recover? Will you take charge of him? Oh, my dear husband! My dear husband!" Leale continued to try to save the president. "His wound is mortal," he finally admitted to Mary. "It is impossible for him to recover."

Lincoln was carried through the

night to a house across the street. Mary followed the men carrying Lincoln's body into the house, barely able to compose herself. When she saw her husband's body, placed at an angle on the small bed so that his feet wouldn't hang over the side, she fell to her knees and begged him to speak to her. In and out of the room she went through the night, often with actress Laura Keene at her side. Mary covered Lincoln with kisses and murmured to him, calling him by name, begging him to speak to her. "Love," she cooed the very last time she saw him, "live but one moment to speak to me once —to speak to our children."

The house in which Lincoln died was across the street from Ford's Theatre.

A distraught Mary Lincoln sobbing at the side of her husband's deathbed

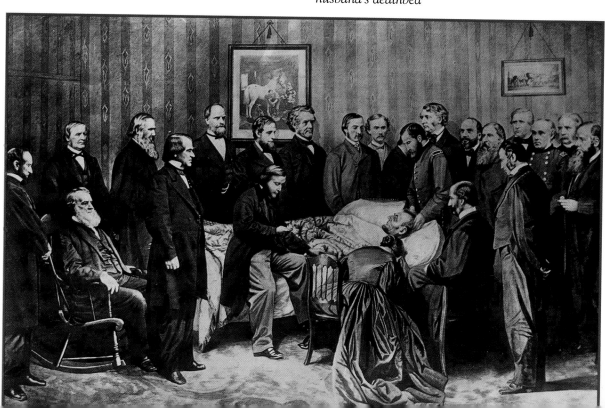

Presidential Assassinations

* *

Including Abraham Lincoln, four American presidents have been assassinated (or murdered) in office. The shock of Lincoln's death must have been extreme because no American president had ever been assassinated before. Sixteen years later, in 1881, Charles Guiteau, a deranged and disappointed office-seeker, wounded President James Garfield in a Washington railroad station. Garfield lingered for more than two months, unable to serve as president. At the Pan-American Exposition in 1901, political fanatic Leon Czolgosz lunged out of the crowd to shoot President William McKinley. McKinley died eight days later, and Czolgosz was executed within two months. John F. Kennedy was gunned down by Lee Harvey Oswald on November 22, 1963, as his motorcade rolled through Dallas, Texas. Unlike these men, no modern president would dream of appearing in public without ample protection. Increased security has foiled recent attempts on presidential lives—including attacks on Presidents Ford and Reagan.

Mary Todd Lincoln had moved to Washington, D.C., and into the White House barely five years earlier with such high hopes. And now, with her husband's assassination, those hopes were dashed. She had tried and failed to impress the capital and the country. She had tried and failed to provide a safe haven for her family. She had tried and failed to be a helpmate to her husband.

As the last few minutes of life faded from her beloved husband, so too did her last moments as First Lady. Her life, which had started with so much promise, was slipping away and, it seemed, there was nothing she could do to stop it.

* * * * * * * * * * * * * * * *

CHAPTER TWO

From Girl to Woman to Marriage

Mary Todd was born in Lexington, Kentucky, on December 13, 1818. Her well-connected and affluent family was deeply committed to the cultural and civic lives of the city. Her father, Robert Todd, was a powerful banker with many important ties in the community. In addition to his business interests, Todd had been elected to public office. He had served at various times through the years as clerk of the Kentucky House of Delegates, councilman, magistrate, sheriff, assemblyman, and state senator.

Lexington was a good-sized southern city, prosperous for a time because of its hemp and cotton indus-

Portrait of America, 1818: An Era of Good Feelings

✯ ✯

So optimistic were Americans in the year of Mary Todd's birth that they referred to the times as the Era of Good Feelings. The War of 1812 had been settled and a firm peace established. The elderly Founding Fathers, having given life and breath to the country during the revolution and in the years following, could now look with pride upon their creation. One of these men was even president: James Monroe would be the last of the revolutionary generation to hold that office.

America could now turn to nation building. The itch to explore and expand spread among a population nearing 9.6 million and growing fast. In the West, the rich lands between the Appalachians and the Mississippi River looked like paradise to this land of farmers. Illinois joined the Union as the twenty-first state, and fur trappers and explorers led the way to the lands beyond. The first steamboat service began on the Great Lakes as a steamer called *Walk-in-the-Water* shuttled between Buffalo and Detroit. And the first great toll road was completed between Maryland and Wheeling, Virginia. To the north, the United States and Britain established most of the Canadian boundary. In the South, so anxious were Americans to take Florida from Spain that military troops used border wars with the Seminole Indians as an excuse to occupy Spanish territory.

Even in the Era of Good Feelings, trouble brewed as Missouri got ready to join the Union. Would it enter as a free state or a slave state? The question was answered with a compromise in 1820: when Missouri entered as a slave state, Maine entered as a free state. But Americans sensed that the question of slavery in an expanding nation would not go away so easily.

As America entered adulthood in 1818, two of its most lasting symbols emerged. Five stars were added to the flag for the last five states admitted, but Congress officially limited the number of stripes to thirteen for the original colonies. In Washington, D.C., Americans admiring the newly painted president's mansion began to call it the "White House" for the first time.

Kentucky, U.S.A.

✶ ✶

By the time Mary Todd was born in Lexington in 1818, Kentucky had long been a state, or "commonwealth," as Kentuckians preferred. Admitted in 1792 as the fifteenth state, its settlement represented the first great pioneering experiment in the young nation. As early as 1767, frontiersman Daniel Boone blazed a trail through the Allegheny Mountains and into the heart of the territory. Pioneers followed close behind. They settled the town of Lexington in 1775 and named it for the Massachusetts village where the American Revolution had just begun. Two years before statehood, "Kentucke" boasted 74,000 inhabitants. Lexington grew rapidly, and during Mary's

childhood, the city was one of the largest and wealthiest west of the Allegheny Mountains. No frontier outpost, Lexington was called "the Athens of the West" for its culture and sophistication. Today, Lexington and the surrounding Bluegrass heartland are famous for horse farms. Mary would have known them as well, since breeding and racing horses began in Lexington around 1805.

Lexington as it looked about 1820.

tries and its large slave market. It began to decline in importance as nearby river cities such as Louisville and Cincinnati grew larger. By the time Mary was born, however, the city was on an upswing and its population was growing.

Robert Todd's enthusiastic embrace of life affected his family, especially little Mary. She and her sisters

21

The house in Lexington, Kentucky, in which Mary Todd grew up

Women of Mary Todd's time were expected to learn how to entertain guests.

and friends attended dances at the city's three dance schools, watched thoroughbred horse races on the city's main streets, heard classical music concerts, and read at the public library, which even had a special children's section. And because of her father's interest in politics—and the fact that Lexington was the county seat—Mary, too, took a keen interest, and often participated in discussions of events of the day.

In this, Mary stood out from the other girls and women with whom she came in contact. In the 1820s and 1830s, women, for the most part, were expected to be interested only in domestic affairs such as decorating, entertaining, and raising children. The rough and tumble of politics, it was

generally thought, was best left to men.

And yet, even though they were responsible for husbands, children, and households, many women had little to do. After all, half the homes in Lexington were run by slaves. By 1830, for instance, Mary's father had one slave for every member of his family—ten slaves cleaned the Todd house and stables, laundered, cooked, tended the children and horses, and shopped for food.

In addition to her family's household slaves and Mammy Sally—her own slave companion who helped raise her—Mary saw the effects of slavery all around her. In fact, one of every three of Lexington's residents was a slave. Mary often saw slaves in chains being

Freedom Train

✶ ✶

Mammy Sally's efforts to help fleeing slaves were part of a vast secret network called the "Underground Railroad." The scheme involved hundreds of people like Sally and Mary around the countryside who quietly helped slaves move and hide until they reached safety in the North and Canada. The term came into use when a slave owner, frustrated by his runaway slave, exclaimed, "He must have gone off on some underground road." Soon slaves all over the South were whispering about the "Underground Railroad." They started using railroad terms: safe houses were "stations" and their owners, "stationmasters." The most dangerous role was that of "conductor." Conductors slipped into the South, helped arrange escapes, and guided slaves ("passengers") along the route to safe stations. The most famous conductor was Harriet Tubman. A slave who ran away on her own, Harriet returned to the slave states to rescue her sister's family who were about to be sold. She escorted more than 300 passengers to freedom using such canny tricks as fleeing south to elude slave catchers. Surely no runaways would head *south!* But the Underground Railroad took any route that led to freedom.

driven down the dusty dirt roads in front of her house. On the way to school, she passed a whipping station. So when Mary helped Mammy Sally hide instructions and bags of food along the way for slaves who were escaping north, and those slaves later stopped at the Todd house to rest, Mary knew enough to be quiet about it.

Besides, Mary had her own problems to deal with. When she was six

Slaves in Southern households cleaned, laundered, cooked, shopped, and tended the children.

Slaves like Mary Todd's companion "Mammy Sally" helped raise children.

years old, the first of many tragedies in her life occurred. Her mother, Eliza, was thirty-one years old. She and Robert had been married a bit more than twelve years. As was common then for most young married women, Eliza was usually either recovering from childbirth or starting another pregnancy. Mary was the Todd's fourth child; her sisters Elizabeth and Frances were older, as was her brother Levi, while Ann, Robert, and George were younger. In 1825, after giving birth to George, Eliza became feverish and died within hours.

As if that weren't distressing enough for such a young girl, within a year of Eliza's death Mary's father remarried. Over the next several years, he and his new wife, Betsy Humphreys, had nine more children.

Life in the Todd house was more crowded and boisterous than ever, with new babies being born every year, it seemed. Worse yet, Mary and her new stepmother didn't like each other. In fact, none of the Todd children liked their new stepmother. Unlike their mother Eliza, who had been shy but loving, Betsy was independent and pretentious. She had an icy stare and dressed plainly, without frills. She and Mary fought often and, not surprisingly given Mary's early interest in fashion, their first big tussle was about clothes.

According to one family acquaintance, Mary—even as a young girl—was "fascinated by the lovely bouffant summer dresses that puffed and swayed so enhancingly on the hoopskirted ladies." But hoops were considered a sign of womanhood, and Betsy thought her nine-year-old stepdaughter was too young to wear such a skirt. Mary thought differently and secretly made one, using willow reeds as a frame. When she paraded in front of her stepmother, Betsy pronounced her a "fright" and ordered her to change. Mary cried, but she wasn't deterred.

Song of the Hoops

* *

Among the most astonishing of nineteenth-century women's fashions was the hoop skirt, popular in the years before 1870. To support the yards and yards of fabric in their flouncy skirts, ladies wore a graduated series of rigid rings, or hoops, hung from their waists. Hoops grew wider and wider as the years went by. In 1857, the popular magazine *Harper's New Monthly* published a witty celebration of the extraordinary fashion that included these lines:

Sailing down the crowded street,
Scraping every one they meet,
With a rushing whirlwind sound,
Muffled belles around abound.
    Hoop! hoop! hoop!
What a vast, expansive swoop!

Hoops of whalebone, short and crisp,
Hoops of wire, thin as a wisp;

Hoops of brass, thirteen yards long,
Hoops of steel, confirm'd and strong;
Sweeping off the public lands,
Turning over apple-stands;
Felling children to the ground,
As they flaunt and whirl around.

    Hoop! hoop! hoop!
What a vast, expansive swoop!

She got back at Betsy by playing tricks on her, such as sprinkling salt in her coffee.

With so many children, and much of Robert Todd's interest focused on his new wife and family, he had less and less time for Mary. She fought for attention, becoming impulsive and stubborn, wanting what she wanted when she wanted it. It wasn't unusual for Mary to throw temper tantrums just to be noticed.

Still, she managed to escape the unpleasantness of her home life by attending social events and school. She was witty and charming and playful by nature. Once, while she was sitting on her front porch, a boy came by and asked her to share some ice cream with him. "I will come if you will wear this wreath of roses," she teased, showing him the wreath she was weaving. He took it from her, placed it atop his head like a crown, and off they went.

For many girls at the time, flirting with boys was a major pastime. It was thought that educated girls were too independent and difficult to marry off. Mary's father, however, disagreed. Unlike many men of his day, he believed that all of his children, not just the boys, deserved the best education money could buy.

In Lexington, that meant Mary studied at Ward's Academy, a strict school that offered a "complete system of female education," and taught math, grammar, and geography along with sewing, painting, and French. She began attending in 1827, the year her father remarried. The school was a three-block walk from her house.

After completing her studies there, Mary entered Mentelle's, a boarding school about 1.5 miles (2.4 kilometers) from her house. The school was run by a French couple. Mary lived on campus during the week and returned to her family on weekends. That first year at Mentelle's, when she was fourteen, her stepmother was pregnant for the fourth time in six years. The house was becoming ever more crowded. At Mentelle's, though it was sometimes a lonely place, Mary received the attention she craved. She did well at her schoolwork, became fluent in French, and acted in French plays.

Years after completing her studies, a friend wrote to Mary's younger half-

"A Complete System of Female Education"

✫ ✫

For the children of Mary Todd's time, going to school was very different than it is today. In 1800, American children received about 200 days of schooling in their entire lives. In the absence of public schools, most children learned at home or at "academies" chartered by the state. Some attended "subscription schools" costing a dollar or two per child. On the frontier, especially, classes were held when teachers were available, most of whom were men. And rarely was attendance required.

For girls, getting an education proved particularly difficult. Many people believed that girls should learn only enough to find husbands and become good wives and mothers. Education beyond that, they felt, would be unbecoming, or worse, disruptive to the family. So girls received a "female education" of music, art, languages, Bible studies, and needlework. College, of course, was out of the question.

However, the ideals of the new nation after the Revolutionary War worked in women's favor. People realized that well-educated mothers would raise more well-rounded children and thereby strengthen the country. In the interest of America's future, women's learning slowly improved. "Female academies" grew popular, and they began to teach a more substantial blend of science, mathematics, and other academic subjects. In 1833, innovative Oberlin College in Ohio even offered a co-educational curriculum, inviting men and women, black or white, to participate.

Meanwhile, the blossoming public-school movement advocated a broad system of free education for all. The first public elementary schools were established in Boston the year Mary was born. In the same city three years later, the nation's first high school was founded. In 1824, the first public high school for girls opened. As public education in the United States got off the ground, the demand for teachers grew and women began to take over this traditionally male profession. In addition to educating their own sons, American women could teach the nation's sons—and daughters. By the time of the Civil War (1861–1865), most American teachers were women. Since 1800, women had gained both an education and a profession.

sister Emilie. In the letter, the friend commented that as a child, Mary had been "bright, sensitive and warmhearted. She was advanced over the other girls of her age in education. We occupied the same room, and I can see her now as she sat on the other side of the table, poring over her books, and I on the other side, with a candle between. She was very studious, with a retentive memory and a mind that enabled her to grasp and thoroughly understand the lessons she was required to learn." But, she said, Mary would change "with every new thought. . . . Her face expressed her varying moods. She would go from happy to sad, from gentle to willful 'Presto!' " Her friend said of Mary's eyes, "They now gleamed with mischief, and before you could be sure of that, her dimple was gone and her eyes were brimful of tears."

In 1833, Mary's older sister Elizabeth had moved to Springfield, Illinois, the state's new capital, and married Ninian W. Edwards. Edwards's father had been the state's governor and, eventually, one of its senators. Her sister Frances had also moved to

Elizabeth Todd
Edwards

Ninian W.
Edwards

Governor Ninian
Edwards

Springfield and through Elizabeth, who was known to be something of a matchmaker, had met and married a doctor there.

Now, in 1839, at twenty years of age, it was Mary's turn to move to Springfield and find a husband. "We had a vacancy in our family," wrote Elizabeth, who went on to say she invited Mary to come to Springfield to make "our home her home."

Though the city had by then been the capital of Illinois for two years, it was a dusty place with unpaved streets and no sewage system. It had a main square with a courthouse, a jail, and a few stores. There were six churches in town, four hotels, and two schools. There were no streetlamps or sidewalks, and cows, pigs, and chickens roamed freely through town. In fact, the city didn't get its first fire engine until 1857.

But because it was the political center of the state, it was teeming with excitement. For a young woman of Mary's grace and intelligence, it was *the* place to be. She was, she admitted, attracted to what she called the "glitter, show, pomp, and power" of the city. She went to a lot of parties and loved to dance, calling it "poetry in motion."

Two years before Mary's arrival in Springfield, a young man named Abraham Lincoln had moved there. His family and background could not have been more different from Mary's. He had been born in 1809 in a one-room log cabin in Kentucky. At age seven,

Abraham Lincoln was born in this log cabin on Nolin Creek in Kentucky.

he had moved with his family to Indiana, "partly on account of slavery," Lincoln recalled many years later. His parents were Baptists and thought slavery was wrong. Because of his family's feelings, Lincoln was, he said, "naturally antislavery" and couldn't even remember a time when he "did not so think and feel." In 1831, while he was in New Orleans, Lincoln saw a slave auction in which a young girl was pinched and prodded and paraded around as if she were a calf. It disgusted him. "By God! If I ever get a chance to hit that institution," he said to a friend, "I'll hit it hard!"

But the Lincolns were poor farmers. They were so poor that their

cabins in Kentucky, and later in Indiana, had dirt floors and bearskins hung in the windows in place of glass. Lincoln slept on a mattress of corn husks and covered himself with a bearskin for warmth. His mother, Nancy Hanks Lincoln, died when he was nine years old.

He had little formal education—less than a year altogether, in fact. "There was absolutely nothing to excite ambition for education," he later recalled. Though his formal education was sporadic, his love of learning was intense. He would hide away for hours—avoiding the farmwork he was expected to do—and read whatever books he could find. "Abe read all the

30

Lincoln's Two Mothers

✫ ✫ ✫ ✫ ✫ ✫ ✫ ✫ ✫ ✫ ✫ ✫ ✫ ✫ ✫ ✫ ✫ ✫ ✫ ✫

Both Abraham Lincoln's birth mother and his stepmother were women of the American frontier. Despite their lack of schooling, these rugged, no-nonsense mothers were able to give both Abe and his sister Sarah a good start in life under difficult circumstances. Nancy Hanks was born in 1784 in Virginia. Upon the death of her father, she and her mother migrated to Kentucky. She and Thomas Lincoln married in 1806. From Nancy, 5 feet, 8 inches (173 cm) tall and slender, Lincoln inherited not only his tall, lanky build, but a love of reading as well. She taught little Abraham the alphabet, and soon he was able to read aloud from the Bible, often the only book in frontier homes. At thirty-five, Nancy died of "milk sickness," which came from the milk of cows that had eaten a certain poisonous plant. The family missed her terribly. When Thomas remarried widow Sarah Bush Johnston, she brought to the family not only her two children, but a new cheer. She was filled with energy, common sense, and affection and, though she was un- schooled, encouraged Abe's reading. They became great friends. Lincoln saw his stepmother for the final time just before his inauguration in 1861. She died in her eighties in 1869.

Abraham Lincoln, *who read whatever books he could find, often had to read by firelight.*

books he could lay his hands on," Lincoln's stepmother, Sarah Bush Johnston, once said. "And when he came across a passage that struck him he would write it down on boards if he had no paper and keep it there until he did get paper—then he would rewrite it. . . . He had a copy book, a kind of scrap book in which he put down all things and thus preserved

Sarah Bush Johnston Lincoln

the same battalion during the Black Hawk War in the early 1830s. In Lincoln's day, local judges traveled twice a year for up to ten weeks on each trip to hear cases in surrounding counties. Lincoln traveled through Morgan, Macon, and Tazewell counties—and others—whenever the opportunity arose. He went from town to town on

Abraham Lincoln and John Todd Stuart opened a law office over a furniture store in Springfield.

them." Eventually, Lincoln learned to read well, and even taught himself some math.

He had moved to New Salem, Illinois, in 1831 and within a year decided to start his political career. He ran for the state legislature. He lost. He ran again in 1834 and won—and won again in 1836 and 1838, the year after he finally moved to Springfield.

By 1836, Abraham Lincoln had finished training as a lawyer and was fully licensed to practice early the following year. Lincoln's first law partner was Mary's cousin, John Todd Stuart, whom he had met while they served in

The Black Hawk War

★ ★

After the American Revolution, a vast expanse of land known as the Old Northwest Territory extended west of Pennsylvania and Virginia and north around the Great Lakes. Congressman Thomas Jefferson recommended that ten new states might be carved out of it. Congress made plans to organize and sell the territory to raise money. But the lands were already occupied by Potawatomi, Miami, Kickapoo, and other Native-American tribes. Through a series of wars, treaties, and relocations, white Americans eventually killed or pushed the native peoples west and opened the lands for themselves. The Black Hawk War of 1832 was the last stand for the tribes of the Great Lakes. Disagreeing with a treaty signed by a rival tribal leader, Chief Black Hawk of the Sauk

Chief Black Hawk

attempted to reclaim his territory along the Rock River in Illinois. He reentered the state with 1,000 men, women, and children. Before long, however, 7,000 U.S. militiamen drove Black Hawk and his people from the land. Those American Indians who had not fled or died from illness or malnutrition were slaughtered at the final bloody encounter in Bad Axe, Wisconsin. While Abraham Lincoln served as a militia captain, he saw no action in the short-lived conflict.

horseback, carrying his papers in saddlebags and, occasionally, even in his stovepipe hat.

Though these trips could be grueling and lonely, Lincoln viewed them as a way to learn and get to know the land and the people. After all, he had political aspirations beyond the state

Lincoln and the court riding the circuit through the counties surrounding Springfield

legislature. Traveling through the nearby countryside gave him the exposure he would need to run for statewide office someday.

At first, he was shy and awkward. Many considered him ugly and ill-mannered. It was no wonder that though he was associated professionally with a relative of Mary's, she did not meet him right away. Mary's sister Elizabeth didn't think Lincoln was "society material."

Eventually, though, Lincoln and Mary attended the same dance and met. He was almost thirty years old. "Miss Todd," he said to her that night, "I want to dance with you in the worst

Mary Todd and Abraham Lincoln were immediately attracted to each other when they met at a fashionable ball.

way." Lincoln, Mary said, was different from the other men she had known. While those men were often sophisticated and charming, Lincoln was brooding and intelligent, Mary thought, and ambitious. He had, she said, "the most congenial mind she had ever met." They became engaged to be married in April 1840.

Mary's sister disapproved of Lincoln and urged Mary to reconsider. In fact, she went so far as to ban Lincoln from her home, making it almost impossible for Mary and Abe to see each other. After all, no respectable young woman would be permitted to spend unchaperoned time with an unmarried man. Lincoln knew of the wealthy Todd family's unhappiness over his relationship with Mary. At one point, he sniffed that one *d* was good enough to spell God, but it took two *ds* to spell Todd.

Still, he began to think that maybe Mary's family was right, Maybe he wasn't good enough for her. Maybe he wouldn't be able to provide for her in the style to which she was accustomed. Nevertheless, Lincoln planned to accompany Mary to a New Year's Eve party, ushering in 1841. But he was late picking her up. She waited. She sulked. And finally she went by herself. When he finally arrived at the party, he saw Mary flirting with another man. According to Mary's sister, Lincoln was "grim and determined" upon seeing her. "Go!" Mary shouted, stamping her foot, "and never, never come back!" Lincoln, sad as could be, left the party.

"I am now the most miserable man living," he wrote soon thereafter.

The estrangement did not last. He and Mary now traveled in similar social circles and saw each other occasionally at parties. Then, sometime in 1842, a mutual friend brought them together. Their romance blossomed once again. It was an election year in Springfield. Their shared interest in politics probably aided their reconciliation. They soon became secretly engaged again.

Mary and Abe planned to be married by the Reverend Charles N. Dresser at his home. But on the morning of the chilly November day they were to wed, Lincoln ran into Mary's brother-in-law Ninian Edwards. He

A typical wedding scene that took place about the time Mary and Abe were married

The State of Illinois,
SANGAMON COUNTY, SS.

THE PEOPLE OF THE STATE OF ILLINOIS,
TO ALL WHO SHALL SEE THESE PRESENTS,—GREETING:

Know Ye, that License and Permission has been granted to any Minister of the Gospel authorized to marry by the Church or Society, to which he belongs; any Justice of the Supreme Court; Justice of any Inferior Court, or any Justice of the Peace, to Celebrate and Ratify the Marriage of Abraham Lincoln & Mary Todd *now both of this county, according to the usual custom and laws of the State of Illinois.*

Witness, N. W. Matheny, Clerk of the County Court, in and for the County of Sangamon, and the Seal of said Court hereunto affixed at SPRINGFIELD, *this* 4th *day of* November *A. D.* 1842

N W Matheny *Clerk*

State of Illinois, } SS.
Sangamon County;

I Certify that, on the 4th *day of* November *A. D.* 1842 *I joined in the Holy State of Matrimony* Abraham Lincoln *and* Mary Todd *according to the custom and laws of Illinois. Given under my Hand and Seal this* 4th *day of* November *A. D.* 1842

Charles Dresser M E

The marriage certificate of Abraham Lincoln and Mary Todd

The Reverend Charles Dresser

confessed to his and Mary's plans. Edwards insisted they delay their wedding by one day so they could marry at his home. Lincoln agreed. So the following night, November 4, 1842, as rain poured down outside, thirty-three-year-old Abraham Lincoln and twenty-three-year-old Mary Todd were wed. They were surrounded by about thirty friends and family mem-

The house in which the Lincolns were married was owned by Ninian W. Edwards.

pairing: She was 5 feet 2 inches (157 cm) tall, plump, with blue eyes, while he was a very slender 6 foot 4 inches (193 cm) tall, with dark brown hair, a long, narrow face, and hollow cheeks. But they were very much in love, which was obvious to all. Lincoln enjoyed Mary's wit and vivaciousness, and she respected his intelligence. He accepted her occasional tantrums, once saying that when she had an outburst he would just leave the house until she calmed down. "It does her a lot of good," he said, "and it doesn't hurt me a bit."

Together, they shared a love of reading and politics, as well as a desire for a family. In fact, Mary often had to defend her choice of him as her mate. "He is a great favorite everywhere," she once said. "He is to be president of the United States someday. If I had not thought so, I never would have married him, for you can see he is not pretty. But look at him! Does he not look as if he would make a magnificent president?"

bers who had been hastily invited. Mary wore a white satin dress and a pearl necklace and was accompanied by two bridesmaids. Lincoln gave her a ring that was engraved with the words "Love is Eternal."

A week later, in a letter to a friend, Lincoln wrote, "Nothing new here, except my marrying, which to me, is a matter of profound wonder."

To some, the couple seemed an odd

☆ ☆ ☆ ☆ ☆ ☆ ☆ ☆ ☆ ☆ ☆ ☆ ☆ ☆ ☆

CHAPTER THREE

Children and the Chance for Glory

* * * * * * * * * * * * * * * * *

Mary may have thought her life with Abe would be a prosperous one. After all, she was married to a man who appeared to be a successful lawyer. That was, at least at first, a very wrong impression.

Though his law firm had been a busy one, often working on more than ten cases a month, its fees were low—usually about $5 a case, and sometimes as low a $2.50. Once he and Stuart charged $50, a fee so high that the client asked if he could pay some of it by making a coat for Stuart.

With marriage, Lincoln realized that he would need to be more financially secure. So he ended his

* * * * * * * * * * * * * * * * *

Lincoln in his Springfield law office, which was located across the street from the state capitol

The newly married Lincolns lived in a room above Springfield's Globe Tavern (above).

partnership with Stuart and joined Stephen T. Logan. Logan was an established attorney with offices across the street from the state capitol and county courthouse. Still, at first his salary didn't allow for the couple to lead a very extravagant life. Their first home together was a $4-a-week room above Springfield's Globe Tavern, a not untypical arrangement for newly-weds.

Mary, who had little experience cleaning and cooking, was forced by necessity to learn. Because she feared that her friends and family would make fun of her, she rarely went out to parties or entertained in her home. Once, when she was a girl, she had asked a friend why it was that "married folks always became so serious." Now, with her new responsibilities, she knew the answer. She even became jealous of her sister Elizabeth, who was

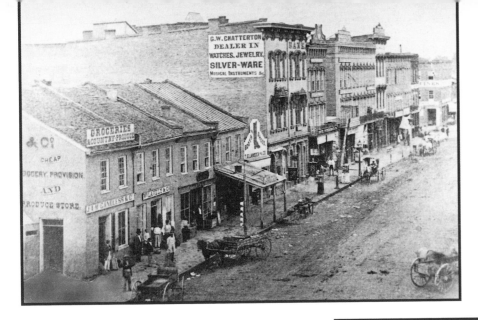

In 1844, when Lincoln formed a partnership with William Herndon, they opened a law office in this block on Springfield Street.

The Lincolns bought this house from Reverend Dresser. (The second floor was added after Tad was born.)

married to a wealthy man. "Mrs. Lincoln was poor and she resented the way people passed her by," said a man who knew both women. "She was hurt and envious."

On August 1, 1843, while the Lincolns were still living at the Globe Tavern, their first child, Robert, was born. He was named after Mary's father. Soon thereafter, Mary recalled seeing Lincoln, her "darling husband . . . bending over me with such love and tenderness." Lincoln, while very much in love, was also working harder than ever. Finally, he and Mary felt confident enough to move. They bought a one-story frame cottage on a small lot on the corner of 8th and Jackson in Springfield. They paid

$1,200 for the house, which they bought from Reverend Dresser, the man who had married them two years earlier.

But memories of Mary's early days of marriage when money was scarce haunted her. At times, she would go out of her way to scrimp and save, while at other times she would spend madly, purchasing fine fabrics, dresses, and jewels, a pattern that would continue for the rest of her life.

In the same way that she had hungered as a girl for attention from her father, she now ached for similar attention from her husband. Lincoln was still traveling for work, leaving Mary alone for up to three months at a time. After giving birth to her second son, Edward, on March 10, 1846, her yearning for Lincoln's companionship grew even more profound. "She was not a model mother," said one observer. "She was too nervous, too impetuous. Her chidings and her caresses depended too much upon her own moods. In times of sickness, she was too anxious and too excitable to be a good nurse." But, he admitted, "she loved her children passionately."

Her loneliness wasn't helped any when Lincoln won a seat in Congress in August 1846. The family moved to a boardinghouse in Washington, D.C. It was located on the spot where the Library of Congress now stands.

Washington, compared to Lexing-

A photograph of Abraham Lincoln, about 1846

ton and Springfield, was an exciting place with its many theaters and lavish parties. It was the type of city in which Mary might have enjoyed living. However, her life in the boardinghouse was far from glamorous. Due to the expense, few congressmen at the time brought their wives and children with them. There, with about ten other congressmen, she was the only

Even though Mary Lincoln was the wife of a congressman and lived in Washington, D.C., she didn't have the time, money, or social status to attend lavish parties such as this presidential reception.

woman and Robert and Edward were the only children. Mary knew few people in town, and with two rambunctious sons to tend to, there was little time to share with Lincoln. It might have been a city of almost 40,000 people, but Mary felt confined.

In 1848, Mary and the boys returned to Springfield without Lincoln in part because, Lincoln said, he thought Mary's presence made it difficult for him to do his job. But soon he missed her sorely. "We are never quite satisfied," Lincoln wrote to Mary a few months after she left Washington. "When you were here, I thought you hindered me some in attending to business; but now, having nothing but business—no variety—it has grown exceedingly tasteless to me." So tasteless, it seems, that Lincoln chose to return to Springfield at the end of his first term and not run for re-election.

His homecoming, however, was marred by young Edward's illness. The boy had become sick a few months before his fourth birthday. At first, the family thought he was suffering from diphtheria, a disease that causes difficulty in breathing, high fever, and weakness. But he stayed sick a long time—much too long for it to have been diphtheria. It became clear as the days passed that Edward was

The Great White Plague

* *

One of the deadliest diseases of Mary Lincoln's time—and for centuries before—was tuberculosis (TB). Although we know today that TB is caused by bacteria that attack the lungs and lymph nodes, nineteenth-century doctors knew nothing of bacteria. Powerless to help, they prescribed bed rest and fresh air. However, these were of little effect against the deadly microbe, which can lurk in the body for years before becoming active. Often called "consumption" because the disease consumes and weakens its victims, its symptoms include a severe cough, difficult breathing, and chest pains. People catch tuberculosis by inhaling the bacteria coughed into the air by those infected, and so it was particularly common in the crowded and unsanitary nineteenth-century cities. In those days before pasteurization, many children contracted a type of tuberculosis that contaminated cow's milk. Although Dr. Robert Koch isolated the tubercule bacterium in 1882, it would take another sixty years for someone to discover an antibiotic to cure the disease. Today, drug-resistant strains of TB are beginning to appear, and 3 million people die of tuberculosis annually around the world.

suffering from tuberculosis, a highly communicable lung disease. In the 1850s, it was the number-one killer of all Americans. In fact, in those days, half the deaths of children under five were due to tuberculosis. Edward died on February 1, 1850.

Mary sank into grief. The funeral was held the day after he died, though Mary probably did not attend. Women of the time rarely expressed grief in public. They hid their grief by staying home and by wearing heavy black mourning clothes and veils if they had to go out. But Mary suffered terribly, staying in bed for weeks afterward, refusing to get up or nourish herself. "Eat, Mary," Lincoln said to her, "for we must live."

Still, their finances continued to improve and slowly Mary began to return to life. She began entertaining a bit and gaining a reputation as a gracious hostess. "I recall the dinner parties given by Mrs. Lincoln in her modest and simple home," wrote one person who had been invited. "There was always a cordial and hearty western welcome which put every guest perfectly at home. . . . It was her genial manners and ever kindly welcome, and Mr. Lincoln's wit, humor, anecdotes, and unrivaled conversation, which formed the chief attraction."

About ten months after Edward's death, on December 21, 1850, Mary gave birth to another son. William was named after Dr. William Wallace, who had married Mary's sister Frances. Three years later, on April 4, 1853, the Lincolns' fourth son was born. With Thomas, named after Lincoln's father, the Lincoln family was complete. The boy was called "Tad" because as a baby, his large, oddly shaped head made him resemble a tadpole.

Lincoln's ambition for higher office

The Lincolns' third son, William (Willie) was named for Dr. William Wallace, the husband of Mary's sister Frances (above).

was rekindled in 1854 with the passage of the Kansas-Nebraska Act. The act reversed the Missouri Compromise of 1820, enacted by Congress to end a series of crises about the extension of slavery into new states and territories. As part of the Missouri Compromise, Maine would be admitted to the Union as a free state and Missouri as a slave state. Slavery was to be prohibited from the Louisiana Purchase northward. But with its repeal, Lincoln and others feared that slavery would spread.

Though Lincoln ultimately failed in his 1854 campaign for the United

Arguments sometimes turned violent during the Kansas Free Soil debate at the Peace Convention in Fort Scott, Kansas.

Huge crowds at the 1858 Lincoln-Douglas debate at Knox College in Galesburg, Illinois

Abraham Lincoln speaking during his campaign for senator against Stephen A. Douglas

States Senate, he was becoming well-known for his antislavery views. In 1858, he ran again for the Senate. His opponent was the current two-term senator, Stephen A. Douglas. Lincoln and Douglas agreed to participate in seven debates across the state. Most of the debates concentrated on the extension of slavery. Douglas believed slavery was an issue that should be decided locally. Lincoln believed it shouldn't be extended at all. By this time, there was no doubt in the public mind that Lincoln opposed slavery.

The founding fathers, Lincoln insisted, said all men were created equal. Even if they themselves owned slaves, they still opposed it in principle, and that was what was important. He had thought the Missouri Compromise was a step in the right direction and that the Kansas-Nebraska Act that repealed it was a great "moral wrong and injustice" because it opened future territory to slavery.

Douglas, a sitting senator, was well funded. He traveled from debate to debate, accompanied by his wife, in a private train car surrounded by aides. Lincoln traveled alone by

Stephen A. Douglas

Left: An ad for the last Lincoln-Douglas debate during the campaign of 1858

ox-drawn wagon. In his absence, Mary campaigned on his behalf, which was unusual for politicians' wives. She wrote letters and referred to the 5 foot 4 inch (162 cm) Douglas as a "very little giant" beside "my tall Kentuckyan." Lincoln traveled 4,200 miles (6,759 km) between August and October. Douglas accused Lincoln of wanting to "extend the Declaration of Independence to blacks," as one historian said. It was during these debates that Lincoln used one of his most famous phrases ever. "A house divided against itself cannot stand," he said, referring to the United States and its increasing division over slavery. Even with such powerful oratory, however, Lincoln lost the election. With this loss, said Lincoln, he would "now sink out of view, and shall be forgotten."

Mary wasn't as accepting—she was furious. She had been determined that he would win and "her anger was so fierce, unreasoning, and permanent," wrote one senator, "that she refused then and ever afterward to speak to the wife of the victor."

Though he had lost both senatorial races, the debates with Douglas had made Lincoln famous throughout the country. In 1860, he ran for president as a Republican.

It was a difficult campaign at a difficult time in the nation's history. The country was literally dividing in two over the issue of slavery, with the South threatening to secede, or leave, the Union and form a confederacy of its own. Because the Democrats could not decide on one candidate, its Northern branch nominated Lincoln's

John C. Breckenridge

John C. Bell

old foe Stephen A. Douglas. The Southern branch put up John C. Breckenridge. Yet a third political party, the Constitutional Unionists, nominated John C. Bell.

An 1860 campaign banner supporting the election of Abraham Lincoln and Hannibal Hamlin

Again, Mary stood out from her female peers by involving herself in Lincoln's campaign. She accompanied him to rallies and wrote letters on his behalf. Because she was witty and talkative and knowledgeable about politics, the press wrote about her in a way they'd never written about any candidate's wife. All this attention only increased her anxiety over the election. Just as she had wanted Lincoln to win when he had run for the

Senate, she wanted him to win this election even more. "I scarcely know how I would bear up under defeat," she wrote. "I trust that I will not have that trial."

Fortunately for them both, she didn't. Lincoln not only won the election that November but upon hearing

1860 campaign newspaper headlines from the Springfield, Illinois, Daily Journal

Opposite: A montage showing President Abraham Lincoln and his cabinet

Jefferson Davis (1808–1889)

✶ ✶

Born in Kentucky a year apart, both Abraham Lincoln and Jefferson Davis also shared the distinction of being presidents in America at the same time. But they were very different men. Davis served in the United States military and in Wash-

ington, including a promising stint as secretary of war under President Franklin Pierce. When the Southern states left the Union, Davis was a U.S. senator from Mississippi. He had discouraged secession, but walked out with his fellow Southerners. His wife Varina, a Washington belle, remembered later that "we felt blood in the air and mourned in secret over the severance of tender ties both of relationship and friendship." Davis became an officer in the Mississippi militia and was chosen president of the Confederacy in February 1861. President Davis took the oath of his office just two weeks before President Lincoln took his. Though not an inspired leader like Lincoln, Davis did his best to guide his new nation with limited resources through the devastating war. Captured at war's end, Davis was held for two years in prison. Working for his release, Varina won only the right to share his cell. After Davis was finally released in 1867, he and Varina lived on the plantation of a friend. Jefferson Davis never regained his U.S. citizenship.

the news, he burst into their house and shouted, "Mary, Mary, we are elected!"

Her happiness was tempered, though, by the knowledge that her own family in Kentucky had not supported her husband for president. They were slave-owning Southerners, after all, and wanted to maintain their way of life. Lincoln's election threatened their future.

A month after the election, before Abraham Lincoln was even sworn in as president, the state of South Carolina seceded from the Union. Six more Southern states quickly followed, forming a new government called the Confederate States of America. Jefferson Davis was its president. Eventually, there were eleven Confederate states in all.

Lincoln, the nation's new president, together with Mary and their three sons, moved to Washington to live in the White House. The Civil War had begun.

☆　☆　☆　☆　☆　☆　☆　☆　☆　☆　☆　☆　☆　☆　☆

CHAPTER FOUR

The First Lady of the Land

★ ★ ★ ★ ★ ★ ★ ★ ★ ★ ★ ★ ★ ★ ★ ★

Any First Lady who presided during the Civil War would have had a hard time of it. What had been for almost three-quarters of a century one nation, indivisible, was suddenly two. The "job" of First Lady, which had up to now consisted mostly of taking care of her family and acting as hostess in the White House, hadn't really changed, but the atmosphere in which she did it was now dramatically different.

Had Mary been First Lady ten years earlier, she might have succeeded in arousing the kind of popularity and social stature for which she pined. Had she been First Lady ten years later, she also might have

★ ★ ★ ★ ★ ★ ★ ★ ★ ★ ★ ★ ★ ★ ★ ★

The White House as it looked during the time Mary Todd Lincoln was First Lady

Union troops being cheered as they leave for the front.

done so. Certainly, her craving to be admired as a hostess and a savvy political helpmate to her husband, as well as a woman of style and grace, would have had a better chance to be realized.

But it was her luck—or, perhaps, her fate—to be First Lady during the bloodiest war the United States had ever seen. Brother was fighting against brother, patriot against patriot.

Life in the White House was supposed to be Mary's triumph. She was the First Lady of the land. Mary was well aware that Washington society was suspicious of any new First Lady, and she was prepared to prove that she was up to the task. In fact, rumors of her crudeness and supposed sympathies for the South preceded her presence in Washington. By the time she

The Civil War: Fast Facts

WHAT: The War Between the States

WHEN: 1861–1865

WHO: Between the Union (Northern states) and the Confederacy (Southern states)

WHERE: Battles fought as far north as Pennsylvania, south to Florida, and west into Missouri

WHY: Many complicated reasons contributed to the outbreak of civil war. Basic differences between the economies and ways of life in the North and the South led to disagreements over slavery and the power of states versus the federal government. When the Southern states left the Union to form their own government, war soon followed.

OUTCOME: After a devastating loss of American life, Northern and Southern, the Union won the war largely because the South ran out of supplies, men, and energy. Slavery was abolished, and the Confederate states returned to the Union.

arrived, she was already facing an uphill battle to win over the city and the country. "The very fact of having grown up in the West," she said, referring to Kentucky and Illinois which at that time were the most western states

Washington at War

✯ ✯

Located at the northern edge of the South, Washington, D.C., occupied a perilous position during the Civil War. Although surrounding Maryland remained loyal to the Union, nearby Virginia seceded just weeks after Lincoln's inauguration. From the White House, the Lincolns could see Rebel campfires burning there nightly. Just across the Potomac River in Arlington stood Confederate general Robert E. Lee's own home, which was quickly taken over by Union troops as war began. In

July 1861, curious Washingtonians even ventured out with picnic lunches to view the battle at Manassas, a bloody defeat for the Union. All the while, Union soldiers streamed into the city, pitching tents in dust and swampland. Some of them even slept on the White House floors. More than 200,000 soldiers passed through during the war, turning Washington into an armed camp. Supply

Stonewall Jackson at the First Battle of Manassas

wagons and ambulances plied the muddy streets, and the wounded crowded makeshift hospitals. While many nervous citizens fled Washington, others came to profit from the chaos, from pickpockets to casket-sellers. Meanwhile, the president insisted that construction continue on the Capitol's dome as a sign that the Union would go on.

A Tough Act to Follow

☆ ☆

It was Mary Lincoln's misfortune to serve as First Lady during the Civil War. What may have been even more discouraging was following in the footsteps of her elegant predecessor, Harriet Lane. The niece of bachelor-president James Buchanan, twenty-seven-year-old Harriet acted charmingly as his official White House hostess from 1857 to 1861. Much admired, Harriet set fashion trends and gave lavish parties. Even as the Civil War drew closer and tensions in Washington mounted, Harriet made a point of inviting guests with political differences to her glittering receptions and dinners.

Mary knew that the fashionable Miss Lane had won the hearts of Washington society and she was anxious to do the same. It was not to be, however. With war in full swing, Mary's extravagant ways seemed hopelessly inappropriate.

Harriet Lane

in the Union, "subjects me to more searching observations."

One of the first things Mary did after Lincoln won his election was to go to New York and buy sixteen dresses, hoping to prove that she as a "Westerner" was as fine and elegant as her eastern counterparts. She loved clothes, especially hoop skirts, low-cut necklines, and long trains, styles then associated with much younger women than Mary. In fact, sometimes even her own husband was surprised by her outfits. Once when he saw her in an

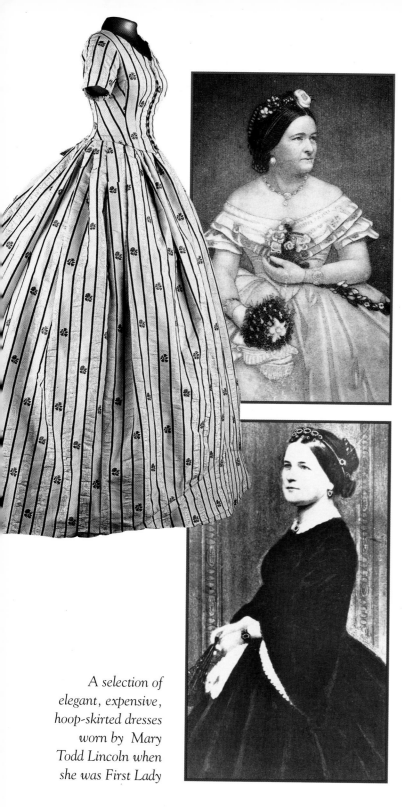

A selection of elegant, expensive, hoop-skirted dresses worn by Mary Todd Lincoln when she was First Lady

extravagant gown with a plunging neckline and satin skirt with a train he said, "Whew! Our cat has a long tail tonight!" and added that "if some of that tail were nearer the head, it would be in better style." However he meant that to sound, his admiration of her was never in doubt. "My wife is as handsome as when she was a girl," he once said of her, "and I, a poor nobody then, fell in love with her; and what is more, I have never fallen out."

Not everyone was so impressed with her extravagance, however. One senator at the time referred to her "bosom on exhibition, and a flowerpot on her head, while there was a train of silk, or satin, dragging on the floor behind her."

Mary ignored such insults. "I intend to wear what I please," she said flatly. But while she thought she was doing the right thing, her critics found much about which to complain. If she dressed poorly, they said, she was behaving vulgarly. If she dressed well, they complained that she was being frivolous and superficial during wartime. American women, wrote one journalist at the time, "sewed, scraped lint, made bandages," while Mary "spent her time rolling to and fro between Washington and New York, intent on extravagant purchases for herself."

Women Pitch In

✫ ✫ ✫ ✫ ✫ ✫ ✫ ✫ ✫ ✫ ✫ ✫ ✫ ✫ ✫ ✫ ✫ ✫ ✫

Women contributed in many ways to the war effort. In both the North and the South, they gathered funds, medical supplies, and clothing for the soldiers. Some women used the opportunity to take the jobs and run the farms that the men had left. On the battlefields, women served as nurses, although they were not encouraged to do so. A handful of women, disguised as men, fought on the front lines for what they believed. As women's roles changed during the Civil War, they learned about independence, self-reliance, and organization. After the war, many women used their new skills to seek equality for themselves.

During her first year in the White House, Mary renovated many of the rooms with a $20,000 allowance from Congress. The building had fallen into disrepair to the point where Mary's cousin Elizabeth Todd Grimsley called it "seedy and dilapidated." Wallpaper was peeling, furniture was broken, and rugs were threadbare. It looked, said her cousin, as if the rooms "were unchanged from George Washington's day." Mary thought if she turned the White House into a showcase, she would impress Washington socialites with her decorating flair. She traveled from New York to Philadelphia buying expensive furniture covered in fabric imported from Paris and draperies

with gold tassels. She bought hand-carved, custom-made furniture as well, and had new gaslights installed. She even paid $1,100 for a set of china embellished with the national seal.

In fact, in her zeal to redo the White House, she overspent her allowance. When Lincoln found out, he was irate and said he wouldn't ask Congress for more money but would instead pay for what she overspent himself. "I'll pay it out of my own pocket first," he said. "It would stink in the nostrils of the American people to have it said the President of the United States had approved a bill over-running an appropriation of $20,000 for 'flub dubs' for this damned old house, when the soldiers cannot have blankets."

The newly decorated White House was the setting for the lavish parties Mary loved to give. In addition to holiday parties, she hosted twice-a-week receptions in winter and spring with as many as 4,000 people crowding into the East Room. One former servant who had worked for five presidents later recalled that the White House was "more entirely given over to the

A plate from the Lincoln china set

The newly decorated White House was the setting for the lavish parties Mary loved to give.

An 1862 New Year's reception at the White House

Mary gave a party at the White House for Prince Napoleon and Princess Clotilde.

This photograph of Mary and her sons Willie (left) and Tad was taken in 1860.

public in Lincoln's administration than in any other."

When Prince Napoleon, the nephew of Napoleon III, emperor of France, came to the United States, Mary gave a party for him. Most everyone spoke French that evening —Mary was fluent in it from her days as a schoolgirl. Napoleon, however, was less than impressed. He called the meal Mary had chosen to serve a bad "dinner in the French style." Fortunately for Mary, the press misunderstood the comment and thought he was complimenting the First Lady. It was one of the few times the press was so generous to her.

This triumph was short-lived, however. As a woman born in the South but now married to a president determined to preserve the Union by *defeating* the South, she was accused by both sides of treachery. After all, Mary's stepmother had sided with the South, as had her brother George and all her half-sisters and all her half-brothers but one. Three of her half-brothers, Sam, Alexander, and David, eventually died defending the South.

"The extreme antislavery elements . . . grew deeply suspicious because Mrs. Lincoln had come from Kentucky," wrote one observer. "Her own brothers and other relatives were living in the South and were serving in the Confederate army. . . . Some people believed that Mrs. Lincoln was a Southern spy in the White House." This Mary could not understand. "Why should I sympathize with the rebels?" she asked. "Are they not against me? They would hang my husband tomorrow if it was in their power. How, then, can I sympathize with a people at war with me and mine?"

But the criticism of those from the South was just as strong. They accused her of treason. "The extreme elements in the South," said one observer, "hated Mrs. Lincoln because she was intensely loyal to her husband and to

Johnny Reb and Billy Yank

☆ ☆

At the beginning of the Civil War, farmers, craftsmen, businessmen, and laborers rushed to enlist in the armies of both the North and the South. Nearly 3 million soldiers served in the war. Among Northern troops, 190,000 were African American. Most troops were between the ages of seventeen and twenty-five, but drummer boys as young as twelve signed up as well. It didn't take much time for the glory of war to turn bitter. Soldiers lived in crowded tent cities when they weren't fighting, marching, or digging trenches. Fierce and deadly battles interrupted weeks of boredom and loneliness. A lack of fresh water and a diet of hardtack (a hard biscuit) and beans led to so much sickness that twice as many men died of disease as from enemy fire. By the end of the war, nearly 620,000 Americans had perished.

General Robert E. Lee and his Confederate troops retreated from the Battle of Antietam.

Union soldiers recapturing artillery during the Battle of Shiloh

Southerner Emilie Todd Helm, Mary's half-sister, was not a gracious guest at the White House.

the Union cause, although of Southern origin."

Mary did, in fact, have strong emotional ties to some of her Southern past. She and Lincoln had both been very fond of her young half-sister Emilie Todd Helm, who was married to Benjamin Hardin Helm, a general in the Confederate army. When he died in December 1863, fighting for the enemy, Mary nonetheless invited Emilie to come stay at the White House

before returning home to Lexington. To get to Washington, D.C., however, Emilie would have to cross through Union-held territory, and therefore swear allegiance to the Union. She refused. Lincoln sent for her personally. Emilie was hardly gracious about Lincoln's generosity. One evening, when a Union general who had lost a leg in the war was visiting the White House, she turned to him and snapped "If I had twenty sons, they would all be fighting yours."

After a few weeks, Emilie left for home, but the damage had been done. Mary was blamed in the press for having allowed the wife of an enemy general to stay at the White House, even if it was her own half-sister.

"I seem to be the scapegoat for both the North and South!" she said. Soon after Emilie returned to Lexington, she wrote Mary a letter in which she blamed Mary and Lincoln for the death of her husband and their siblings. Mary never saw or spoke to Emilie again.

This separation was made all the more difficult because it came on the heels of her beloved son Willie's ill-

The city of Washington, D.C., as it looked from the dome of the Capitol in 1860

ness and death. Washington, with a population of about 65,000 by the time the Lincolns returned there to live in the White House, swelled to almost 200,000 people as the war progressed. Water mains broke under the stress of so many people and sewage flowed into the Potomac River, from which most drinking water came.

In February 1862, both Tad and Willie became ill. As Tad began to recover, however, eleven-year-old Willie grew worse. He cried and moaned through the night, and his shrieks of pain could be heard throughout the White House. Mary watched as he grew thinner and thinner and suffered

The Lincolns' son Willie, who had contracted typhoid, died in 1862.

68

from diarrhea and cramps. He had contracted typhoid fever from contaminated water.

Though she loved all her children, Willie was Mary's favorite because he was most like Lincoln himself: spirited, generous, kind, and intelligent. His death hit Mary hard.

Once again she displayed—or rather, didn't display—her grief as most women in her day did: She stayed away from any public ceremonies, such as his funeral. It was said then that "visible emotion" only showed a woman's "lack of faith in the doctrine that the dead passed from this world into God's better one."

After Willie's death, Mary suffered a nervous breakdown and stayed in her room, as she had when Edward died. For three months, she stayed in bed in anguish, sobbing and holding herself against the emotional pain. She even screamed out for Willie to return. "The fairest are most frequently taken from a world of trial for some wise purpose, which we cannot understand," Mary later wrote in a letter to a friend. Though she wanted to believe the sentiment, she found it hard to find a place for it in her heart. She was in too much anguish. With Willie's death, wrote Mary's cousin, "had gone part of the doting mother's heart also, which was never more to find peace and comfort, mourning and refusing to be comforted."

Lincoln, afraid his wife might go insane, one day pointed out the window to a building in the distance where mental patients lived. "Try to control your grief," he told her, "or it will drive you mad, and we may have to send you there."

Still, even the sound of Willie's name often sent her into fits of sobbing. She gave away all his toys and clothes and she never again went into the room where he had died or into the Green Room where his coffin had lain. She was so crushed by his death that even five months later she could barely write about "our crushing bereavement." For a long time afterward, she said, his death would enter her mind and that thought would send her into a deep sadness for days.

Willie's death, however, did have another effect on the First Lady. It made her stronger against her attack-

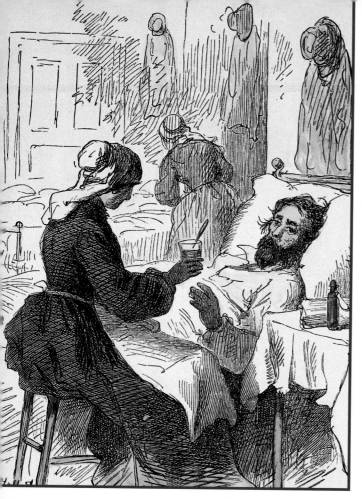

Mary brought food and flowers to injured soldiers in hospitals, read to them, and wrote letters for them.

ers. "I used to shed many bitter tears [about being criticized]," she said, "but since I have known real sorrow—since little Willie died—all these shafts have no power to wound me."

Through it all—the controversies about the White House redecorating, her clothing, and even her sympathies regarding the war—Mary still did not understand completely why she was so despised. After all, she was doing what she thought a First Lady should do. There was a war raging, after all, and Mary didn't ignore it. She brought food and flowers to injured soldiers in hospitals, read to them, wrote letters for them, and once raised $1,000 for the Christmas dinner at a military hospital. She also supported the Contraband Relief Association, founded in 1862, which raised money to help slaves who came to the North during the war. "It may not be known that Mrs. Lincoln has contributed more than any other First Lady . . . from her private purse to alleviate the suffering of our wounded soldiers," wrote one sympathetic newspaper at the time.

Mary also took up various causes, chief among them, abolition. After all, her seamstress and friend Elizabeth Keckley had been born a slave and wasn't able to buy her freedom for twenty-five years. Through conversation with her and memories of her girlhood "Mammy," Mary turned firmly against slavery. Mary was the first First Lady to entertain black Americans in the White House. She

Elizabeth Keckley (c. 1818–1907)

✯ ✯

"Lizzie" Keckley was probably Mary Todd Lincoln's closest friend. Born a slave in Virginia, Lizzie worked hard as a seamstress for the Garland family's five daughters and caring for her own son George. After the Garlands moved to St. Louis, Lizzie met and married James Keckley, a scoundrel whom she soon left. A quiet and determined woman, Lizzie taught herself to read and write and borrowed $1,200 to purchase freedom for herself and George in 1855. She moved to Washington, where her skill as a seamstress earned her a following of distinguished customers and eventually the business and trust of Mary Todd Lincoln. More than the First Lady's maid and seamstress, Lizzie became a loyal companion with whom Mary shared her most personal opinions and feelings. In 1868, Lizzie wrote a book called *Behind the Scenes, or Thirty Years a Slave, and Four Years in the White House.* Although she intended her book to win sympathy for the increasingly unstable Mrs. Lincoln, it earned Lizzie no friends. She never saw Mary again and passed the remainder of her life in declining circumstances. Though not well received in its time, Lizzie's book has been a rich resource for historians hoping to know and understand Mary Todd Lincoln better.

even allowed a black Sunday School group to use the South Lawn for a picnic, an act that was considered extremely controversial at the time.

Mary also tried to fulfill her desire to be a help to the president, offering him advice whenever possible. "The country may congratulate itself upon the fact that its president is a man who does not reject, even in important

A hand-colored etching of President Abraham Lincoln

matters, the advice and counsel of his wife," wrote *The New York Times*.

Just as often, though, Mary sought to do favors for people who had given her gifts or had done favors for her in the past, especially if those gifts or favors were inducements for her to speak to the president or some other member of his administration on their behalf. One man gave her diamonds and afterward Mary asked Lincoln to give him a job with a naval agency—and he did. Another gave her a black carriage and four black horses before the inauguration, hoping to be granted special treatment. Just as Lincoln became known for *not* taking gifts, Mary became known for the opposite—those seeking her help waited to see her in the upstairs hall through which she had to walk to go to her room. After she saw someone, she would write letters to the appropriate person asking for help. "Allow me to intercede with you . . . ." she would write, or "Will you not confer a favor upon me. . . ."

The difficulty of Mary's life in Washington only served to make her many insecurities worse. She and the president received many death threats through the mail and Mary began to get extremely nervous whenever Lincoln was out of her sight. She was jealous of other women and had tantrums over the tiniest of errors or what she perceived to be social slights. "It was not easy at first to understand why a lady who could be one day so kindly, so considerate, so generous, so thoughtful and so hopeful, could, upon another day, appear so unreasonable, so irritable, so despondent and so prone to see the dark, the wrong side of men and women and events," said one of the president's assistants.

Like other First Ladies before and after her, Mary was chiefly concerned with the safety and well-being of her family. The war was a long and lonely experience for the president, and Robert, Tad, and Willie (until his death) were a great comfort to him. He found them "antidotes" to the overwhelming melancholy of the war. The house itself was alive with their

This portrait of Lincoln's family includes, from left to right, the president (sharing a book with Willie), Tad, Robert (standing at back) and Mary.

joyful laughter, not to mention the romping of their many pets, including kittens, rabbits, a turkey, a goat that slept in Tad's bed, and a dog named Jip that slept on the president's lap. The Lincolns, it seemed, couldn't do anything right. Even allowing their children the freedom to enjoy their childhood drew criticism. They were spoiling them, it was said. But the Lincolns didn't care. "Let them have a good time," they said. There would be more than enough time later on to grow up.

After Willie's death, one of Mary's greatest fears was losing another son. In his late teens, Robert was at an age where he should have been in the army. Mary, however, was deathly frightened of his going away and never coming back. Robert, a student at Harvard University, wanted to leave school and enter the army. Mary was dead set against it. But Lincoln was president and, it was asked, shouldn't the president's son be expected to go to war and risk his life as had the sons of so many others? The pressure continued. The matter was settled when Robert enlisted and joined the staff of

Robert Todd Lincoln left Harvard to enlist and join the staff of Union General Ulysses S. Grant.

Lincoln appointed Ulysses S. Grant as general-in-chief of all the Union armies in March 1864.

General Ulysses Grant, far from the front lines to ensure his safety.

The war dragged on from year to year. As the president geared up for re-election in 1864, Mary had her own agenda. Yes, the country needed Lincoln in the White House to finish and finally win the war. It needed Lincoln to unite it once again. But beyond that, Mary needed him to be reelected for far more selfish reasons. She was many thousands of dollars in debt for dresses and other finery she had charged without Lincoln's knowledge.

In fact, she owed $27,000 to various shopkeepers—a lot of money today, and an enormous amount back

President Lincoln visited General George B. McClellan at Antietam, Maryland, in 1862.

ABRAHAM LINCOLN.
FOR PRESIDENT

A. JOHNSON.
FOR VICE PRESIDENT

An 1864 campaign poster supporting Abraham Lincoln for president and Andrew Johnson for vice president

President Lincoln reading a book with his son Tad

then. If Lincoln lost the election, he would find out about her spendthrift ways and, she told her seamstress, "he will know all." There was no telling where his anger would lead. But if he won, Mary went on, "I can keep him in ignorance of my affairs." Those to whom she owed money would not want to insult her by demanding payment right away. She might be able to pay her debts without Lincoln ever finding out.

Not only that, but if her mountain-high debt became public during the campaign, Lincoln's enemies might use it against him in the election. Lincoln did win, but Mary had learned

Lincoln and Tad arriving in Richmond, Virginia, after the Confederates were evacuated in April 1865, shortly before Lincoln's assassination

This lithograph is a depiction of the Lincolns' last White House reception, which took place not long before the president was asssassinated.

nothing from the fear of disclosure she had felt. In fact, for the president's second inauguration, Mary spent $2,000 on a new ball gown.

Still, she was anxious. Prone to premonitions, she kept having the same dream over and over, that Lincoln was shot dead in front of her. She dreamed she was at his funeral. She could see herself there, weeping at his graveside. In fact, one day soon after the reelection she made yet another expensive purchase—$1,000 worth of mourning clothes.

She was of two minds about the future. Yes, she was having nightmares. Yet there were good dreams and hopes, too, that she and Lincoln might find great happiness and togetherness after the war was won and after he retired. They had talked of traveling through Europe and to California together, of doing so many things.

But that was never to be. Her worst nightmare *did* come true: Lincoln was shot to death before her very eyes. More than half of her own family had died—William and Edward, and now her beloved husband.

The death of the president was pure agony for Mary. She couldn't face it and, just as when her sons had died, wasn't expected to. From her bedroom window in the White House she could

Henry Ward Beecher delivering the funeral oration at the White House on April 19, 1865

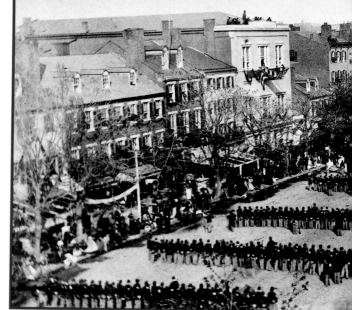

Lincoln's funeral procession began in Washington, D.C. (above).

see the coffin being carried away. She could imagine the polite eulogies, though she did not hear them. She could imagine the murmurs of grief, but she did not listen. She stayed in her room, locked inside not by a key but by her own anguish.

With Robert already an adult living on his own, Tad felt the brunt of his mother's sadness. "Don't cry so, Mama! Don't cry!" Tad pleaded once as he threw his arms around his mother's neck, "or you will make me cry too! You will break my heart!"

Mourners lined the track as Lincoln's funeral train took the president from Washington, D.C., across the country to Springfield, Illinois, where he was buried.

Tad Lincoln in uniform after Secretary of War Edwin M. Stanton gave him an officer's commission

wrote to Mary, "what your suffering must be."

After Lincoln died, Mary slowly began to give some of his belongings away to people who had been close to the couple. She gave two of his canes to the black abolitionists Frederick Douglass and H. H. Garnet and she gave the blood-stained dress she had worn the night Lincoln was killed to

Queen Victoria of England sent a letter of condolence to Mary after Lincoln's death.

Mary received thousands of letters from around the world expressing sympathy, but one in particular meant the most to her. Queen Victoria of England's husband, Prince Albert, had died in 1861 and her bereavement over his death had affected her greatly. She hid away at Windsor for many years afterward. "No one can better appreciate than I can who am myself utterly *broken hearted* by the loss of my own beloved husband who was the *light* of my life, my stay—*my all,*" she

Bound for Glory

✯ ✯

The violent death of President Lincoln shook the nation to its roots, the terrible news coming just as people celebrated the end of the Civil War. A national spirit of mourning gripped the land. Grieving Americans wore pins and badges proclaiming their sadness: "A Nation Mourns the departed patriot, statesman, and martyr." Posters lamented "a martyred father!" Black bunting veiled homes and businesses. Perhaps the best measure of the nation's sorrow came along the route of Lincoln's funeral train as it rolled slowly from Washington to Springfield, Illinois. The carefully planned twenty-day journey retraced the route Lincoln had taken to his first inauguration in 1861, stopping in Baltimore, New York, Indianapolis, Chicago, and other cities along the way. For 1,700 miles (2,736 km), mil-

Lincoln's burial at Oak Ridge Cemetery

lions of people turned out to watch the eight railroad cars carrying the bodies of Lincoln and his son Willie (who had died several years before and was to be buried with his father) pass slowly by. In the designated cities, Lincoln's body was removed from the train and escorted with great ceremony to lie enshrined for public viewing. Even in the worst weather, people thronged to pay their respects or catch a glimpse of the fallen leader. Arriving in Springfield on May 4, 1865, father and son were laid to rest at Oak Ridge Cemetery. Overcome by her grief, Mary Lincoln was not among the three hundred mourners who accompanied Lincoln on his final journey.

Mary gave one of Lincoln's canes to abolitionist Frederick Douglass.

had won the war and united the country once again, virtually no one came to pay her a visit, or their respects. "It was not strange that Mrs. Lincoln was not able to leave the White House for five weeks after her husbands death," said one journalist. "It was her misfortune that she had so armed public sympathy against her, by years of indifference to the sorrows of others, that when her own hour of supreme anguish came there were few to comfort [her]."

In fact, in the weeks after the assassination during which Mary continued to live in the White House, the only "visitors" were thieves, who raided the mansion stealing anything they could get their hands on, including the curtains. Mary, it seemed, was all alone. "The silence," said Keckley, remembering those last weeks in Washington with Mary, "was almost painful."

her good friend and seamstress, Elizabeth Keckley.

But the silence in the White House was more than she could bear. Though she had been the First Lady of the land, the wife of the president who

★　★　★　★　★　★　★　★　★　★　★　★　★　★　★

CHAPTER FIVE

The Years of Mourning

✫ ✫ ✫ ✫ ✫ ✫ ✫ ✫ ✫ ✫ ✫ ✫ ✫ ✫ ✫

For the first time in her life, Mary was homeless. But worse, she was frightened. She not only felt penniless, but she also knew she owed large sums of money. With the president no longer alive, those to whom she owed the money would come after her.

Before she could think about what to do, however, she needed to find a home. Her son Robert was by now a lawyer in Chicago and that seemed the natural place for her to go.

On May 23, 1865, Mary and Tad left the White House for good. Wearing heavy black drapery, she waited for the train at the nearby depot. "It was so

✫ ✫ ✫ ✫ ✫ ✫ ✫ ✫ ✫ ✫ ✫ ✫ ✫ ✫ ✫

After they left the White House, Mary and Tad went to Chicago, where Robert (above) was living.

unlike the day when the body of the president was borne from the hall in grand and solemn state," recalled her friend Elizabeth Keckley, who waited with Mary. "Then thousands gathered to bow their heads in reverence as the plumed hearse drove down the line . . . now the wife of the president was leaving the White House and there was scarcely a friend to tell her good-bye. The silence was almost painful."

Upon her arrival in Chicago, Mary lived in various hotels and boarding-houses, but life there was expensive. Regardless of the amount of money she actually had, which was considerable for the times, she *felt* that she didn't have enough, certainly not enough to repay her debts and live in a style she felt she deserved. Lincoln had died with no will, so by law what money and possessions he had were divided equally among Mary and her two surviving sons, Robert and Tad.

Mary felt the country *owed her* a better future. She demanded that Congress pay her the remainder of Lincoln's four years' salary, which would have been about $100,000. Congress, however said no. First of all, many of its members said, there was no previous case in which it had voted for such a measure for a president's widow. Secondly, the actual amount Lincoln left, which totaled about $85,000, was well known. In the end, Mary was given the remainder of one year's salary, about $22,000. Mary complained bitterly that such an amount would not be enough to purchase a new house. "Besides, she wrote in a letter, "we would require to have it furnished and means to keep it up—

Union Station in Chicago about the time Mary and Tad Lincoln arrived in 1865

A view of Randolph Street as it looked about the time Mary Lincoln was in Chicago

what a *future* before us—the wife and sons of the Martyr President *compelled* to be inmates of boardinghouses all their lives."

Whether it was rational or not, Mary panicked over money. Because of the debtors from her past to whom she owed money and Tad and herself whom she had to support in the future, she saw little hope. Unfortunately, one of the ways she thought to raise money turned out to bring "down on her such a spate of criticism," said one historian of the 1867 debacle, "that she was ultimately forced to flee the country in humiliation."

As a grief-stricken widow who dressed solely in heavy black crepe dresses and veils, Mary decided she no longer needed her many fancy ball gowns, furs, and hats. "I might as well turn them into money, and thus add to my income," Mary said. "It is humiliating to be placed in such a position, but as I am in the position I must extricate myself as best I can."

The idea seemed simple enough—the public would flock to buy the clothes once worn by the much-admired president's wife. She traveled to New York under a false name, Mrs. Clarke, so no one would know what she was up to. She was to meet her friend Elizabeth Keckley there and arrange the sale. Both heavily veiled to hide their identities, they met on a park bench in Union Square Park to discuss the plans. Her behavior might have been almost comical if it weren't so sad and pathetic.

Mary Lincoln and Elizabeth Keckley met on a park bench in New York City's Union Square Park (right) in 1867 to discuss plans to sell Mary's gowns.

But once the public learned that the clothes belonged to the former First Lady, it turned on her with a vengeance. People came to gawk and pick at the clothes but not to buy. When the sale itself failed, she planned to send her clothes, including the blood-stained dress she wore the night of Lincoln's assassination, on tour. Only the fact that the authorities in Providence, Rhode Island, the tour's first stop, refused to give its permission, prevented the tour from taking place.

After this fiasco, the Cincinnati *Commercial* called Mary "an intensely vulgar woman," while the *Springfield* (Massachusetts) *Republican* referred to her as "that dreadful woman . . . in the open market with her useless finery" who "persists in forcing her repugnant individuality before the world." "Mrs. Lincoln has dishonored herself, the country, and the memory of her lamented husband," wrote the *Albany Journal*. "No doubt Mrs. Lincoln is deranged—has been for years past, and will end her life in a lunatic asylum," said a letter to the editor in the *New York Tribune*.

Former First Lady Mary Todd Lincoln as she looked about 1869

What was supposed to be a glittering success was yet again another failure for Mary. Dejected and alone —and now more in debt than ever, since she had lost money trying to arrange the sale—she returned to Chicago. "I am so miserable I feel like taking my own life," she said.

By the following year, Mary had had enough. She and Tad, then fifteen years old, sailed for Europe. There, she thought, she might not only live less expensively, but be paid more respect for whom she had been and who she was now, the widow of the slain presi-

In Europe, Mary enrolled Tad in a boarding school in Frankfurt, Germany (above).

dent of the United States. She left Chicago to escape what she called "persecution from the vampire press."

In Europe, Mary enrolled Tad in a boarding school near Frankfurt, Germany. He was a sweet boy, comforting to her and thoughtful. "Taddie is like some old woman with regard to his care of me," she wrote to one friend. "His dark, loving eyes watching over me remind me so much of his dearly beloved father's."

Mary took a room nearby and saw Tad often between her travels around the Continent, including England, Italy, France, and Scotland. But even in Europe, away from the vicious treatment she had experienced in the United States, she could find no peace. Back home, she had been wag-

Tad Lincoln

While Mary Todd Lincoln was in Europe from 1868 to 1871, she toured England's Windsor Castle (left), Glasgow, Scotland (below), Paris (bottom), and Italy.

ing a war to receive an annual pension from Congress. She had asked for $5,000 a year at a time when even generals' wives were receiving only $600 a year. Mary's request languished in Congress—though it was reported in the European press—due mostly to her unpopularity with its members. Finally, however, both Congress and the Senate approved a $3,000 pension, not as much as she had wanted, but enough for her to feel she had at least won a small part of the battle.

Feeling somewhat confident over winning the pension from Congress, she and Tad sailed home in March 1871. Aboard ship, however, Tad caught a terrible cold. For six months, Mary stayed in Chicago with Robert's family as she tried to nurse Tad back to health. Nothing she did, it seemed, helped. Tad was only eighteen years old when he died, most likely of tuberculosis, on July 15, 1871. Mary was fifty-three.

Yet again, Mary was plunged into extraordinary sorrow. She believed that people were out to get her. She became afraid of the dark, even refusing to blow out the candles in her rooms. She began to hallucinate, and suffered migraine headaches. She carried thousands of dollars on her at all times, in her petticoats. "I feel there is no life for me, without my idolized Taddie," she said. "One by one, I have consigned to their resting place my idolized ones, and now, in this world, there is nothing left me, but the deepest anguish and desolation."

Mary continued to travel extensively over the next few years, unable or unwilling to settle anywhere for long. She was fearful of poverty and though Robert was healthy, she worried that he was ill. She visited spiritualists often, hoping to learn what would happen to her and her family in the future, and even attended seances to speak with the dead. She lived simply in rented rooms or hotels, always carrying her money with her.

When Mary returned to the United States with her very ill son Tad, she stayed with Robert (above).

Robert's wife, Mary Harlan Lincoln

In 1875, Mary—whose behavior was growing odder—stayed in a Chicago hotel for a brief time. Robert, visiting her there, entered her room and found her only partly dressed. Still not completely covered, she left the room and, Robert said, "The next I knew of her she was going down in the elevator to the office. I had the elevator stopped, and tried to induce her to return to her room."

Robert, embarrassed by his mother's increasingly erratic behavior, decided to take action. He claimed she was insane and wanted to have her committed to a hospital or a sanitar-

Robert Todd Lincoln (1843–1926)

☆ ☆

Before the age of forty-one, Robert Lincoln lost his three younger brothers, lived through his father's assassination, and watched his mother's sad mental decline. In spite of those hardships, Robert built a normal and quiet life for himself. While his mother insisted that he graduate from Harvard as the Civil War raged, Robert yearned to join the army. After graduation in 1864, his father found him a post with General Grant where he would be safe yet useful. As a member of the general's staff, Robert was present at Appomattox Courthouse when Lee surrendered. He returned from the army on April 14, 1865, and turned down his father's invitation to the theater that fateful night. After the assassination, Robert went on to practice law in Chicago. He married a senator's daughter in 1868 and they had three children: Mary, Abraham, and Jessie. Robert was reluctant to enter politics or trade on the Lincoln name, but he did accept appointments as secretary of war and as minister to England. He also enjoyed a successful career in business as an officer of several corporations. By coincidence, Robert was nearby during the assassinations of two other presidents. On his way to see James Garfield in 1882, he received word that the president had been shot. When, bound for Buffalo in 1901, he heard that President McKinley had been attacked in that very city, Robert hurried to his bedside.

ium. "I do not regard it safe to allow her to remain longer unrestrained," he said. "She has long been a source of great anxiety. She has been of unsound mind since the death of her husband, and has been irresponsible for the last ten years. I regard her as eccentric and unmanageable."

Mary, humiliated by her son's accusations, went on trial. "She had strange imaginings, thought that someone was at work on her head, and that an Indian was removing the bones from her face and pulling wires out of her eyes," one doctor who had examined Mary told the court. "She complained that someone was taking steel springs from her head and would not let her rest."

It was a fast trial and it took the jury only ten minutes to return a guilty-of-insanity verdict. "We the undersigned jurors in the case of Mary Todd Lincoln," said the jury, "having heard the evidence in the case, are satisfied that Mary Todd Lincoln is insane, and is a fit person to be sent to the state hospital for the insane. . . ."

As she was dragged away, she screamed at Robert. "Oh, Robert! To think that my son should ever have done this!"

Life at the hospital in Batavia, Illinois, was dreary. Mary complained of never being left alone without an attendant, of bars on her windows, or of her personal possessions being stolen. She decided to fight for her freedom, and demanded another trial. She hired a lawyer, Myra Bradwell, who was the first female lawyer in the state, and working together with her sister Elizabeth, Mary was granted a new trial. Mary, Bradwell told the court, was "no more insane than I am." This time, the court agreed with Mary, and

Mary's sister, Elizabeth Todd Edwards

Myra Bradwell (1831–1894)

☆ ☆

Mary Lincoln's friend, the energetic and resourceful Mrs. Bradwell, worked tirelessly for legal and social reforms, equal rights for women, and other progressive causes. As founder and publisher of the *Chicago Legal News*, she also proved herself to be a shrewd businesswoman, building her publication into a respected and important law journal. Her witty commentary on the legal world was widely read. She used her pen to urge the passage of laws to reform business, zoning, and the legal profession itself. In 1869, Myra Bradwell passed the Illinois bar exam to become a lawyer, but the court refused to grant her a license "by reason of the disability imposed by your married condition." In response to her appeal, the court again denied her, this time because she was a woman. Undaunted, she rededicated herself to her reform-minded journalism. Though she never reapplied to practice law, the court granted her a license in 1890, shortly before her final battle with cancer. With her husband, attorney James Bradwell, she had befriended the Lincolns during trips to Springfield in the 1850s. Mary wrote of their relationship in the last years of her life: "When all others . . . failed me in the most bitter hours of my life, these loyal hearts, Myra Bradwell and her husband . . . rescued me. . . ."

Mary's son Robert committed her to Bellevue Place, a mental hospital in Batavia, Illinois.

set her free. She was, the court pronounced, "restored to reason."

Mary's final few years were spent traveling in the United States and Europe, suffering from diabetes, migraine headaches, and arthritis. In between her travels, she would spend long periods of time living in her sister Elizabeth's house in Springfield, in a dark room with the shades drawn throughout the day. In July 1882, while at her sister's, Mary had a stroke and died. She was sixty-four years old.

Regarding Abraham and Mary Lincoln, the Reverend James A. Reed, who officiated at Mary's funeral, said that ". . . they had virtually both been killed at the same time. With the one worked for them in factories, sweatshops, and mines. They labored long hours for low wages, often under dangerous and dirty conditions. These workers organized unions and sometimes used strikes and violence to push for reforms and better working conditions. The first Labor Day celebration took place in 1882, a sure indication of the rising voice of the working class.

Between the rich and the poor arose a new middle class with leisure time to fill. Bicycle riding, handball, and a new sport for men and women called croquet quenched a thirst for fun. Brand-new spectator sports such as baseball, boxing, and college football captured the public fancy. Americans loved to learn, too, and colleges around the country admitted more students than ever before. Even women, long excluded from higher education, attended college in record numbers.

Inventions and improvements came thick and fast. On the farm, in the home, and at work, new devices and appliances made life easier and more efficient. On September 4, 1882, Thomas Edison threw the switch on the world's first commercial electric power plant in New York City. For the first time, 59 buildings lit up with 400 incandescent bulbs. Following soon were the first electrically lit Christmas tree, the first hydroelectric plant, and the first electric railway company. Soon, all of America would bask in the new electric light.

that lingered, it was slow death from the same cause. So it seems to me today that we are only looking at death placing his seal upon the lingering victim of a past calamity."

Mary Todd Lincoln was an extraordinary woman living in extraordinary times. She fought for—and suffered because of—her independence and intelligence. Never before had there been a First Lady like her. It would be years before other First Ladies would assert such independence again.

Though she was judged a failure by many historians, Mary Todd Lincoln had nevertheless paved the way for many modern American First Ladies to come.

The Presidents and Their First Ladies

President	Birth–Death	First Lady	Birth–Death
YEARS IN OFFICE			
1789–1797			
George Washington	1732–1799	Martha Dandridge Custis Washington	1731–1802
1797–1801			
John Adams	1735–1826	Abigail Smith Adams	1744–1818
1801–1809			
Thomas Jefferson†	1743–1826		
1809–1817			
James Madison	1751–1836	Dolley Payne Todd Madison	1768–1849
1817–1825			
James Monroe	1758–1831	Elizabeth Kortright Monroe	1768–1830
1825–1829			
John Quincy Adams	1767–1848	Louisa Catherine Johnson Adams	1775–1852
1829–1837			
Andrew Jackson†	1767–1845		
1837–1841			
Martin Van Buren†	1782–1862		
1841			
William Henry Harrison‡	1773–1841		
1841–1845			
John Tyler	1790–1862	Letitia Christian Tyler (1841–1842)	1790–1842
		Julia Gardiner Tyler (1844–1845)	1820–1889
1845–1849			
James K. Polk	1795–1849	Sarah Childress Polk	1803–1891
1849–1850			
Zachary Taylor	1784–1850	Margaret Mackall Smith Taylor	1788–1852
1850–1853			
Millard Fillmore	1800–1874	Abigail Powers Fillmore	1798–1853
1853–1857			
Franklin Pierce	1804–1869	Jane Means Appleton Pierce	1806–1863
1857–1861			
James Buchanan*	1791–1868		
1861–1865			
Abraham Lincoln	1809–1865	Mary Todd Lincoln	1818–1882
1865–1869			
Andrew Johnson	1808–1875	Eliza McCardle Johnson	1810–1876
1869–1877			
Ulysses S. Grant	1822–1885	Julia Dent Grant	1826–1902
1877–1881			
Rutherford B. Hayes	1822–1893	Lucy Ware Webb Hayes	1831–1889
1881			
James A. Garfield	1831–1881	Lucretia Rudolph Garfield	1832–1918
1881–1885			
Chester A. Arthur†	1829–1886		

† wife died before he took office   ‡ wife too ill to accompany him to Washington   * never married

1885–1889			
Grover Cleveland	1837–1908	Frances Folsom Cleveland	1864–1947
1889–1893			
Benjamin Harrison	1833–1901	Caroline Lavinia Scott Harrison	1832–1892
1893–1897			
Grover Cleveland	1837–1908	Frances Folsom Cleveland	1864–1947
1897–1901			
William McKinley	1843–1901	Ida Saxton McKinley	1847–1907
1901–1909			
Theodore Roosevelt	1858–1919	Edith Kermit Carow Roosevelt	1861–1948
1909–1913			
William Howard Taft	1857–1930	Helen Herron Taft	1861–1943
1913–1921			
Woodrow Wilson	1856–1924	Ellen Louise Axson Wilson (1913–1914)	1860–1914
		Edith Bolling Galt Wilson (1915–1921)	1872–1961
1921–1923			
Warren G. Harding	1865–1923	Florence Kling Harding	1860–1924
1923–1929			
Calvin Coolidge	1872–1933	Grace Anna Goodhue Coolidge	1879–1957
1929–1933			
Herbert Hoover	1874–1964	Lou Henry Hoover	1874–1944
1933–1945			
Franklin D. Roosevelt	1882–1945	Anna Eleanor Roosevelt	1884–1962
1945–1953			
Harry S. Truman	1884–1972	Bess Wallace Truman	1885–1982
1953–1961			
Dwight D. Eisenhower	1890–1969	Mamie Geneva Doud Eisenhower	1896–1979
1961–1963			
John F. Kennedy	1917–1963	Jacqueline Bouvier Kennedy	1929–1994
1963–1969			
Lyndon B. Johnson	1908–1973	Claudia Taylor (Lady Bird) Johnson	1912–
1969–1974			
Richard Nixon	1913–1994	Patricia Ryan Nixon	1912–1993
1974–1977			
Gerald Ford	1913–	Elizabeth Bloomer Ford	1918–
1977–1981			
James Carter	1924–	Rosalynn Smith Carter	1927–
1981–1989			
Ronald Reagan	1911–	Nancy Davis Reagan	1923–
1989–1993			
George Bush	1924–	Barbara Pierce Bush	1925–
1993–			
William Jefferson Clinton	1946–	Hillary Rodham Clinton	1947–

Mary Todd Lincoln
Timeline

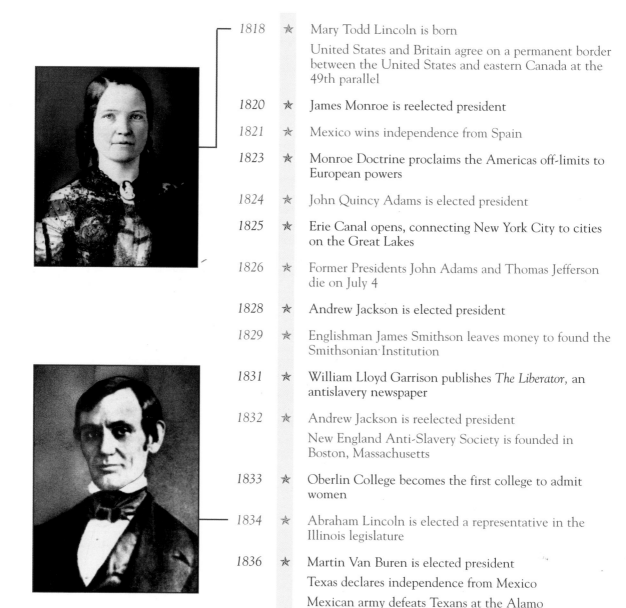

1818	★	Mary Todd Lincoln is born
		United States and Britain agree on a permanent border between the United States and eastern Canada at the 49th parallel
1820	★	James Monroe is reelected president
1821	★	Mexico wins independence from Spain
1823	★	Monroe Doctrine proclaims the Americas off-limits to European powers
1824	★	John Quincy Adams is elected president
1825	★	Erie Canal opens, connecting New York City to cities on the Great Lakes
1826	★	Former Presidents John Adams and Thomas Jefferson die on July 4
1828	★	Andrew Jackson is elected president
1829	★	Englishman James Smithson leaves money to found the Smithsonian Institution
1831	★	William Lloyd Garrison publishes *The Liberator,* an antislavery newspaper
1832	★	Andrew Jackson is reelected president
		New England Anti-Slavery Society is founded in Boston, Massachusetts
1833	★	Oberlin College becomes the first college to admit women
1834	★	Abraham Lincoln is elected a representative in the Illinois legislature
1836	★	Martin Van Buren is elected president
		Texas declares independence from Mexico
		Mexican army defeats Texans at the Alamo

1837 ✷ Economic depression spreads throughout the United States

1838 ✷ Native Americans are forced from the southeastern United States to present-day Oklahoma; many die along the Trail of Tears

1839 ✷ Mary Todd moves to Springfield, Illinois

1840 ✷ William Henry Harrison is elected president

1841 ✷ William Henry Harrison dies a month after taking office and John Tyler becomes president

1842 ✷ Massachusetts supreme court recognizes labor unions

Massachusetts passes laws regulating child labor

Mary Todd marries Abraham Lincoln

1843 ✷ Robert Lincoln is born

1844 ✷ James K. Polk is elected president

1846 ✷ United States declares war on Mexico

John Deere constructs a steel plow

United States annexes New Mexico from Mexico

Oregon Territory is divided between United States and Great Britain at the 49th parallel

Edward Lincoln is born

Abraham Lincoln wins a seat in the U.S. House of Representatives

1847 ✷ U.S. Army captures Mexico City

Maria Mitchell is the first woman elected to the American Academy of Arts and Sciences

Smithsonian Institution is formally dedicated

1848 ✷ Treaty of Guadalupe Hidalgo ends the Mexican War and gives most of the present-day Southwest to the United States

First U.S. women's rights meeting is held in Seneca Falls, New York

Gold is discovered in California

First medical school for women is opened in Boston, Massachusetts

Zachary Taylor is elected president

1850	★	Zachary Taylor dies and Millard Fillmore becomes president
		Edward Lincoln dies
		William (Willie) Lincoln is born
1852	★	Franklin Pierce is elected president
		Harriet Beecher Stowe's *Uncle Tom's Cabin* is published
1853	★	United States acquires the rest of the present-day Southwest through the Gadsden Purchase
		Thomas (Tad) Lincoln is born
1854	★	Republican Party is formed
		Kansas-Nebraska Act allows the two territories to decide for themselves whether or not to allow slavery
1856	★	James Buchanan is elected president
1858	★	First trans-Atlantic wire is laid between Great Britain and the United States
		Abraham Lincoln debates Stephen Douglas during the campaign for a U.S. Senate seat from Illinois
1860	★	Abraham Lincoln is elected president
		South Carolina secedes from the Union
1861	★	Confederate States of America (eleven seceded Southern states) is formed
		Confederates fire on Fort Sumter, starting the Civil War
		President Lincoln calls for volunteers to serve the Union
1862	★	Confederate army defeats Union forces at the Second Battle of Bull Run and at Fredericksburg
		William (Willie) Lincoln dies
1863	★	President Lincoln issues the Emancipation Proclamation
		Union forces defeat the Confederacy in major battles at Gettysburg and Vicksburg
		President Lincoln gives the Gettysburg Address
1864	★	Union general William Tecumseh Sherman captures Atlanta
		Abraham Lincoln is reelected president

1865	☆	Confederate general Robert E. Lee surrenders to Union general Ulysses S. Grant at Appomattox Courthouse
		Abraham Lincoln is assassinated
		Andrew Johnson becomes president
1867	☆	United States purchases the Alaska territory from Russia
1868	☆	President Johnson is impeached but not removed from office
		Ulysses S. Grant is elected president
		Louisa May Alcott's *Little Women* is published
1869	☆	First professional baseball team, the Cincinnati Red Stockings, is formed
1871	☆	Chicago Fire destroys most of that city
		Thomas (Tad) Lincoln dies
1872	☆	Ulysses S. Grant is reelected president
		Yellowstone National Park is established
1873	☆	San Francisco installs a cable car system
1875	☆	Mary Todd Lincoln spends four months in a mental institution in Batavia, Illinois
1876	☆	General George Armstrong Custer and his troops are killed at the Battle of the Little Big Horn
		Alexander Graham Bell invents the telephone
1877	☆	Rutherford Hayes becomes president
		Thomas Edison patents the phonograph
1879	☆	Women win the right to argue cases before the U.S. Supreme Court
1880	☆	James A. Garfield is elected president
1881	☆	James A. Garfield is shot and dies
		Chester A. Arthur becomes president
1882	☆	Congress approves a pension for all widows of U.S. presidents
		Mary Todd Lincoln dies on July 16

Fast Facts about
Mary Todd Lincoln

Born: December 13, 1818, in Lexington, Kentucky

Died: July 16, 1882, in Springfield, Illinois

Burial Site: Springfield, Illinois

Parents: Robert Smith Todd and Eliza Parker Todd; stepmother Betsy Humphreys Todd

Education: Ward's Academy, where she studied math, grammar, geography, French, sewing and painting; Mentelle Boarding School, where she became fluent in French and acted in French plays

Marriage: To Abraham Lincoln on November 4, 1842, until his death on April 15, 1865

Children: Robert (1843–1926), Edward (1846–1850), William (Willie) (1850–1862), Thomas (Tad) (1853–1871)

Places She Lived: Lexington, Kentucky (1818–1833); Springfield, Illinois (1833–1846, 1848–1861; various times 1875–1882); Washington, D.C., (1846–1848, 1861–1865); Chicago, Illinois (1865–1868, 1871); various places in Europe (1868–1871); various places in the United States (1871–1875; 1875–1882); Batavia, Illinois (May–September 1875)

Major Achievements:

　⋆ Held public receptions twice a week in the East Room, allowing thousands of people to enter the White House.

　⋆ Comforted soldiers injured in the Civil War by bringing food and flowers to them in hospitals, by reading to them, and by raising $1,000 for a Christmas dinner at a military hospital.

　⋆ Worked for the abolition of slavery and supported the Contraband Relief Association, which aided slaves who moved to the North during the Civil War.

　⋆ Was the first First Lady to entertain African Americans in the White House.

Fast Facts about
Abraham Lincoln's Presidency

Terms of Office: Elected in 1860 and reelected in 1864; served as the sixteenth president of the United States from 1861 until his death on April 15, 1865, from assassination on April 14, 1865.

Vice Presidents: Hannibal Hamlin (1861–1865); Andrew Johnson (March 4, 1865–April 15, 1865) who became president of the United States when Abraham Lincoln died.

Major Policy Decisions and Legislation:

* Proclaimed that an insurrection existed between the states and called for the states to send troops for the U.S. Army and Navy (April 15, 1861).
* Signed income tax act (August 5, 1861) and Internal Revenue Act (June 30, 1864), which increased the income tax.
* Signed act that abolished slavery in Washington, D.C. (April 16, 1862).
* Signed the Homestead Act (May 20, 1862), which offered land in the West for $1.25 per acre (per .04 hectare).
* Issued the Emancipation Proclamation (January 1, 1863).
* Issued first national Thanksgiving Day proclamation on October 3, 1863.
* Signed act that prohibited slavery in the territories (June 19, 1862).

Major Events:

* The Civil War began (April 12, 1861) when the Confederates fired on Fort Sumter in South Carolina.
* The U.S. Senate confirmed all four of President Lincoln's associate justice of the U.S. Supreme Court appointments: Noah Haynes Swayne (January 24, 1862), Samuel Freeman Miller (July 16, 1862), David Davis (December 8, 1862), and Stephen Johnson Field (March 10, 1863).
* President Lincoln delivered the Gettysburg Address on November 19, 1863, to honor the soldiers who died in the Battle of Gettysburg.
* The U.S. Senate confirmed President Lincoln's appointment of Salmon P. Chase as chief justice of the U.S. Supreme Court (December 6, 1864).
* The Civil War ends (April 9, 1865) when General Robert E. Lee surrenders to General Ulysses S. Grant at Appomattox Courthouse, Virginia.

Where to Visit

The Capitol Building
Constitution Avenue
Washington, D.C. 20510
(202) 225-3121

Lincoln Boyhood National Memorial
P.O. Box 1816
Lincoln City, Indiana 47552
(812) 937-4541

Lincoln Home National Historic Site
413 South Eighth Street
Springfield, Illinois 62701-1905
Visitor Center: (217) 492-4241 ext. 221

Lincoln Memorial
National Capital Parks-Central
The National Mall
900 Ohio Drive, S.W.
Washington, D.C. 20242
(202) 426-6841

The Lincoln Museum
200 East Berry Street
P.O. Box 7838
Fort Wayne, Indiana 46801-7838
Phone: (219) 455-3864
Fax: (219) 455-6922

Museum of American History of the
    Smithsonian Institution
"First Ladies: Political and Public Image"
14th Street and Constitution Avenue
    NW
Washington, D.C.
(202) 357-2008

National Archives
Constitution Avenue
Washington, D.C.
(202) 501-5000

The National First Ladies Library
The Saxton McKinley House
331 S. Market Avenue
Canton, Ohio 44702

White House
1600 Pennsylvania Avenue
Washington, D.C. 20500
Visitor's Office: (202) 456-7041

White House Historical Association
740 Jackson Place NW
Washington, D.C. 20503
(202) 737-8292

Online Sites of Interest

The First Ladies of the United States of America
http://www2.whitehouse.gov/WH/glimpse/firstladies/html/firstladies.html
A portrait and biographical sketch of each First Lady plus links to other White House sites

Ford's Theatre National Historic Site
http://www.nps.gov/foth/link.htm
Discussion of the assassination, a photo gallery, many links to specifics of the assassination, and more

Internet Public Library, Presidents of the United States (IPL POTUS)
http://www.ipl.org/ref/POTUS/alincoln.html
An excellent site with much information on Abraham Lincoln, including personal information and facts about his presidency; many links to other sites including Mary Todd Lincoln, Lincoln biographies, and other Internet resources

Lincoln Boyhood National Memorial Lincoln City, Indiana
http://www.nps.gov/libo
Description of the Visitor Center and bookstore, the Lincoln Living Historical Farm, and tours of the park

Lincoln Home National Historic Site Springfield, Illinois
http://www.nps.gov/liho/
Includes history, a tour with photos, and links to much Lincoln information

The National First Ladies Library
http://www.firstladies.org
The first virtual library devoted to the lives and legacies of America's First Ladies; includes a bibliography of material by and about the nation's First Ladies and a virtual tour, with pictures, of the restored Saxton McKinley House in Canton, Ohio, which houses the library

The White House
http://www.whitehouse.gov/WH/Welcome.html
Information about the current president and vice president; White House history and tours; biographies of past presidents and their families; a virtual tour of the historic building, and much more

The White House for Kids
http://www.whitehouse.gov/WH/kids/html/kidshome.html
Information about White House kids, past and present; famous "First Pets"; historic moments, a newsletter, and more

For Further Reading

Anderson, Lavere. *Mary Todd Lincoln: President's Wife*. New York: Chelsea House Publishers, 1991.

Biel, Timothy. *The Civil War*. San Diego: Lucent Books, 1991.

Chang, Ina. *A Separate Battle: Women and the Civil War*. New York: Lodestar Books, 1991.

Collins, David R. *Shattered Dreams: The Story of Mary Todd Lincoln*. Notable Americans series. Greensboro, N.C.: Morgan Reynolds, 1994.

Gormley, Beatrice. *First Ladies*. New York: Scholastic, Inc., 1997.

Gould, Lewis L. (ed.). *American First Ladies: Their Lives and Their Legacy*. New York: Garland Publishing, 1996.

Jacobson, Doranne. *Presidents and First Ladies of the United States*. New York: Smithmark Publishers, Inc., 1995.

Klapthor, Margaret Brown. *The First Ladies*. Washington, D.C.: White House Historical Association, 1994.

Marrin, Albert. *Commander in Chief: Abraham Lincoln and the Civil War*. New York: Dutton Children's Books, 1997.

Mayo, Edith P. (ed.). *The Smithsonian Book of the First Ladies: Their Lives, Times, and Issues*. New York: Henry Holt, 1996.

Meltzer, Milton (ed.). *Lincoln in His Own Words*. Orlando, Fla.: Harcourt Brace & Company, 1993.

Murphy, Jim. *The Long Road to Gettysburg*. New York: Clarion Books, 1992.

O'Neal, Michael. *The Assassination of Abraham Lincoln*. Great Mysteries, Opposing Viewpoints series. San Diego: Greenhaven Press, Inc., 1991.

Rutberg, Becky. *Mary Lincoln's Dressmaker*. New York: Walker and Company, 1995.

Sandak, Cass R. *The Lincolns*. New York: Crestwood House, 1992.

Wilkie, Katherine E. and Leslie Goldstein. *Mary Todd Lincoln: Girl of the Bluegrass*. Childhood of Famous Americans series. New York: Aladdin Paperbacks, 1992.

Index

Page numbers in **boldface type** indicate illustrations

Photo Identifications

Cover: Portrait of Mary Todd Lincoln by Katherine Helm
Page 8: An 1864 photograph of Mary Todd Lincoln by Mathew Brady
Page 18: The earliest known photograph of Mary Todd, taken when she was twenty-eight
Page 38: An 1861 portrait of Abraham and Mary Todd Lincoln
Page 54: Color portraits of Mary Todd Lincoln and Abraham Lincoln
Page 82: A photograph of Mary Todd Lincoln wearing black

Photo Credits©

About the Author

Dan Santow is a former producer of *The Oprah Winfrey Show* and writer at *People* magazine. He is the author of *The Irreverent Guide: Chicago* (Frommer's/Macmillan, 1996) and has been published in many magazines, including *Redbook, Town & Country, Metropolitan Home, Men's Health, Chicago* magazine, the *Chicago Tribune Magazine*, and *Advertising Age*, among others. Mr. Santow is a graduate of Vassar College and holds a master's degree in journalism from Northwestern University. He lives in Chicago.